CONTENTS

INTRODUCTION

GETTING MARRIED. What does it all mean? You will have your own ideas, and only you can decide its special significance. But this is what a group of sixteen-year-old school leavers thought:

> 'It's a new beginning, a chance to start again, but this time it's sharing.'

> 'It's floating down the aisle in a filmy white dress and feeling like Princess Diana just for once, with everyone looking at you.'

> 'It's swearing to love, honour and obey. It's a sort of vow, really. I don't fancy having to do what I'm told – I don't think I'll bother about that bit.'

> 'It's something that costs a lot of money and it's hard when your Dad's not got a job.'

> 'It's being happy and sad at the same time – you know you wouldn't *not* want to do it, but you're frightened because things will never be the same again.'

> 'It's the most important day in your life; it's a ceremony to remember for ever and ever. It's what songs sing about, poets write about, and advertisements tell you about.'

Like most of their age group, these girls thought that marriage was still 'a good thing' – even though one of them had recently heard a vicar remind the congregation that a third of modern marriages end in divorce. 'It's right to have a warning – it makes a wedding much more serious', they agreed. And a wedding is indeed a serious ceremony, a celebration, a public performance with you as the

getting
MARRIED

getting MARRIED

ALMA WILLIAMS

WARD LOCK LIMITED · LONDON

With love and thanks to Yvonne and Bill
whose wedding provided the inspiration for this book.

ACKNOWLEDGEMENTS

The author and publishers would like to thank the following for kindly providing photographs for the book:

Laura Ashley Ltd, page 63; Camera Press Ltd, pages 1, 43, 70; Katherine and Nicholas Davies-Twaite/John Macleod, Photographic Services, Liverpool, page 59; Jo and Laurie Kurtland/Peter Dyer Photographs Ltd, Enfield, Middx, pages 58, 74, 82; Sheila Macqueen/Roy Smith, page 51; Stella and Roger Mayo/Eric Standing, Photographer, Maidstone, Kent, pages 26, 90; Moss Bros of Covent Garden, page 47; Transworld Features, pages 7, 15, 19, 22, 30, 66, 67, 71, 75 (left and right), 79, 95; Jo and Rod Westrop/Evening Post-Echo Ltd, page 94.

The cover photograph and those on pages 3, 11, 35 and 83 were taken by Tom Mannion; hair by Anthemos of Crimpers (Hampstead); make-up by Casey; the wedding gown was loaned by Pronuptia.

©Alma Williams 1984

First published in Great Britain in 1984
by Ward Lock Limited, 82 Gower Street,
London WC1E 6EQ, a Pentos Company.

Filmset in Monophoto Bembo
by Latimer Trend & Company Ltd, Plymouth

Printed and bound in the Netherlands by
Comproject BV Holland

British Library Cataloguing in Publication Data

Williams, Alma
Getting married.
1. Weddings
I. Title
395'.22   HQ745

ISBN 0-7063-6302-7

'It's being happy and sad at the same time.'

star, but yet personal and private. There is love and laughter, romance and ritual, dreams and drama, tears and even fears, combining mysteriously and magically to make this the most moving and memorable experience of your life. 'But this time it's sharing.'

A memorable experience? If you ask your grandmother about her wedding day, she will be able to tell you down to the last detail about the scuff marks on her white glacé kid shoes, the exact number of tiny, hand-made buttons at the back of her dress, the lace-edged lavender-scented hanky she passed over for her mother to cry into in the vestry – and all about Uncle George who got disgracefully drunk at the reception. You too will store up your memories and pass them on with old faded photographs and pressed rose-leaves to your grandchildren. But people often forget to remind you that quite small things can spoil this most important day, replacing your warm glowing feeling with tears, irritation and even anger. You cannot stop your family version of Uncle George getting drunk if he is really determined, but there are many steps you can take to make your service, ceremony and celebration momentous – and memorable. The point of this book is to help you in your plans and preparations to recognize the importance at every stage of choosing, making conscious decisions, and checking.

The problem is that when you have fixed your wedding day there are so many things you need to know, so many questions you want to ask. You are excited but uncertain, afraid of your own ignorance and inexperience. If you come from an average-sized family, your parents will not have had much opportunity for planning and organizing weddings. Your mother will rely on her memories of a generation ago, when the situation was different. And you? You will have looked on at your friends' weddings, perhaps even participated as a bridesmaid, but always as an observer, without the responsibility for making those key decisions.

In order to make decisions you have to make a list of your own – and your family's – needs, preferences and priorities, and then match them up with what is available. It all sounds easy enough in theory, but in practice there are obstacles in your way as soon as you start to choose and decide: time and money – both may be short, and access to reliable information difficult. It is not that there is a shortage of information in books and magazines, rather that there is so much of it. You become bewildered and befuddled by all the facts that are shouted out at you and all the advice that friends and relations shower upon you. It must be *your* wedding, a wedding for sharing, a wedding with the stamp of your personality upon it, not a mass-produced package-deal of a wedding.

A memorable experience – and a commercial experience. From the moment when you first announce your engagement you will become aware of the industry built up around weddings; vast sums are involved, with millions of pounds spent each year on getting married. This relatively new industry will virtually ignore your future husband except for trying to press life insurance upon him, but you will become a mini-employment bureau with everyone everywhere trying to persuade, flatter, cajole, even manipulate you into buying their goods and using their services. You have been conditioned since you were a little girl by attitudes and advertisements, by what 'the songs sing about and the poets write about' into certain expectations: a traditional wedding with all the expensive accessories; a long white dress, a lavish reception, a fleet of chauffeur-driven cars, an ivory leather wedding album. Fine, if these are things that you really want after you have compared a range of similar services and looked objectively at products on the market. For even the filmiest of wedding gowns is still only a *product* that somebody has made, and it still needs to be assessed in the same way as a car, a carpet or a kettle. But the dress is packaged as a dream and it is hard to separate dreams from reality, or indeed to stop dreams from becoming nightmares. With stars in your eyes, it is so very easy to make a hasty judgement which is not necessarily going to give you that day of delights. You are likely to fall victim to your emotions: 'You deserve the best', 'Why settle for second best?', 'Nothing but the best is good enough for you on your wedding day' the advertisements tell you. And they are right. But what does 'best' mean? It all depends on how you choose to interpret it; and 'best' does not necessarily mean the most expensive. Sometimes something made with love is the best and that costs nothing: a Victorian posy of flowers from a cottage garden, with rosemary, myrtle and southernwood, or a fine lawn camisole, hand-made, with delicate drawn-threadwork. These are the symbols of something that commerce cannot provide and money cannot buy. On the other hand, 'the best' for you may turn out to be a wedding organized from start to finish by a firm of experts, if that is what you need, want and can afford. Choice in all its variations exists. What are *you* going to choose and how are you going to get what you want within the constraints that every bride has to accept one way or another? What compromises, what alternatives are possible? Choice, constraint and compromise: these are the central themes of this book.

How will you use the book? Maybe you will start by skimming through, looking at the pictures, each one chosen to illustrate a particular and often practical point. It is not necessarily a book to be read through from cover to cover; it is a book to have around, a book to cherish and to keep, a book to be dipped into, and then studied as your needs arise. The check-lists and suggestions are there to be ticked off as the right moment comes up, to prompt and remind you. The intention is not to over-organize you; you are not staging a play or planning a military manoeuvre, though there will be moments when you feel as if you are. Rather, the book sets out to provide practical guidelines, to start off trains of thought which spark off ideas of your own. It is a book full of examples and real stories of resourcefulness, ingenuity and imagination which will help you to get the best value for the money you choose to spend, to realize how vulnerable you are to emotion, persuasion and other people's pressures, and to sort out the problems that are bound to occur.

The wedding day you create will be yours, personal and individual, but shared; a day that will be all that you want it to be, for in you lies the power to make it what you want it to be. Maxim Gorky said that 'getting married is like jumping into a hole in the ice in the middle of winter: you do it once, and you remember it for the rest of your days.' This book can take the chill off the water as you take your jump into the unknown.

1
COPING WITH COSTS

HOW MUCH WILL IT ALL COST?

IF YOU want a traditional white wedding with all the trimmings, your final bill will probably reach an astonishing four figures. Princess Diana's wedding cost over £570,000. You may feel like a princess on your wedding day, but you do not have to spend that amount of money in order to make it the happiest of days. Getting married is actually very cheap, one of the best bargains there is: for the price of a licence and your bus fare to the register office, you are able to make the most solemnly binding of promises. Nevertheless most girls want more than this, aspiring to a church ceremony and consequent celebrations.

For this reason, the rapidly-expanding wedding industry provides a vast range of goods and services to tempt the 350,000 couples who get married in Britain each year. You are in a new world, choosing and rejecting things you never knew existed before you became a bride. Do you want a commissionnaire to salute you as you arrive at the church? Would you like a scribe to write your wedding invitations in an elegant long-hand? Or a silver-plated Wilkinson sword to cut your cake with, as a highlight to the reception: a sword polished and etched with horseshoes, bells and orange-blossom? Maybe not, but you are likely to need cars to get you to the ceremony of your choice, special-occasion clothes, flowers, a reception for your guests and a record of the event. And these are the items which, one way or another, can climb up to between £1000 and £1500. The total cost of a wedding depends on how much you are willing to spend, and on how much you are prepared to shop around to get exactly what you want.

WHO PAYS? A POLICY FOR FAMILIES

In the past, the burden of paying has fallen pretty heavily on the father of the bride, who inherits the dowry tradition: the bridegroom confers an honour on the bride's family by marrying her, and he has to be rewarded. This is why the word 'wedding' is linked in its origins with 'wage'. So, in the past, fathers have

'It's floating down the aisle in a filmy white dress and feeling like Princess Diana just for once, with everyone looking at you,'

been expected to pay for the wedding dress, bridesmaids' dresses, press announcements, invitation cards, most of the cars, photographs, flowers for the church and reception, and the reception itself. The groom's side of the family have got off lightly, paying only for the wedding ring, the church or register office fees, flowers for the bride, bridesmaids and mothers, transport for himself and his bride after the ceremony, and for the honeymoon. But there are now few families who keep strictly to this traditional arrangement, which does not fit in with the idea that women occupy an equal place in society. The royal family, though for different reasons, paid for much of Princess Diana's wedding.

As soon as an engagement is announced, there must be a family discussion about how much money is going to be available. On this depends the sort and size of wedding: whether the dress will be second hand, sale bargain or Christian Dior creation; whether the guest list can be extended to include Great Aunt Sarah who drinks tea out of her saucer, as well as the Honourable Douglas McLaughlin; whether the reception will be at the Grosvenor, the local pub, cricket pavilion or on the back lawn.

You may even question the wisdom of spending any money at all, apart from the bare minimum, on a one-day performance. It is always important to ask yourself quite bluntly, 'What else could we do with the money?' Perhaps it would be better spent on longer-term investments, like a house, a car, or furniture and labour-saving equipment. Perhaps it would be better saved, to provide security for your parents in retirement or redundancy. It all depends on how highly you value your day as princess, the life-long memories, the symbolic launching into a new life. What price are you prepared to pay for the satisfaction of your emotions? How in fact do you balance price and value? Oscar Wilde once defined a cynic as someone who knew the price of everything but the value of nothing!

The debate is for you and your family, but discussion and decision are not easy because at every step you are all influenced by the external pressures of society, tradition, and commerce. Fathers, as well as daughters, are the targets for advertisements: 'Surely you don't begrudge your daughter on this the greatest day of her life . . .?' is the preface to an advertisement designed to arouse feelings of guilt if daddy does not comply with the accepted idea of duty towards his daughter. It is not, therefore, unknown for a father to press upon his daughter the whole of his redundancy money: Daphne was engaged and her wedding day fixed when her father lost his job after thirty years in the printing industry. With tears in his eyes he handed over his lump sum. It was, he thought, her birthright, his final investment in her future and the visible proof of his love. With tears in her eyes and a lump in her throat Daphne accepted his generosity, conditioned like him by attitudes and advertisements. For them no other decision was possible. But were they right or were they wrong? The final choice might turn out to be the right one for them, though the process of getting there could be wrong. Did they stop to ask, 'What else could be done?', listing other possibilities, balancing price and cost, which are objective and tangible, against value, which is subjective and intangible; or did they jump into an instant, instinctive and unreasoned decision?

Most families tend to avoid realistic, reasoned discussions about money, and many adult children have no idea of their parents' income and prospects. Even within one family, disposable income can be a taboo subject. Yet now, two families, perhaps still unknown to each other, are expected to talk freely about money. And if there is not at this stage a getting together, a willingness to admit and be honest, hurt pride, grudges and resentment can sour the start of a new life. So a clear policy of some sort is necessary, making the wedding much more of a shared event, involving a wider circle of family and friends, with contributions in kind valued as much as those in cash. It is total resources that count, not just money. And people are resources. Great Aunt Sarah, for example, may sip her tea rather noisily, but she can still make a good fruit cake and she was once awarded a City and Guilds Certificate in cake icing; Mrs Johnson next door works at the local florist and would be glad to get the flowers at cost; Mr Price will offer his Peugeot family estate car to ferry people from church to reception.

Parents who may be facing a difficult and uncertain situation at work may want to contribute, but be happier to put a named and predictable sum into a family 'pool', rather than have bills they have forgotten all about – like the photographer's – trickling in for weeks and even months after the wedding. They also have to take into account fairness to other children in the family. Do they all get an identical sum or should the amount for later marriages be increased to take inflation into account? Do sons get treated in the same way as daughters? And what about a child who decides not to get married at all?

It can happen that a young couple with a joint income may be earning more than either set of parents and are prepared to pay for the style of wedding they want. Mary and Michael are both graduates and trained accountants, but Mary's father is facing premature retirement while Michael's parents are both already living off their old age pension. Mary's and Michael's problem is not the level of their salaries or indeed of their future security; their worry concerns their immediate cash flow since they have not been working long enough to build up capital for a house deposit and for the outgoings of a medium-sized wedding. How do they solve their problem without giving offence to either family?

Open, friendly discussion reveals that Mary's parents want to provide £300 in cash and a deep-freezer for a wedding present, and her mother wants to buy her daughter's wedding dress out of the fifty-pence pieces she has been saving up in a jam jar. They are also in a position to make a short-term, interest-free loan for a year as their own financial problems will not catch up with them for a while yet. Michael's family have no cash to give or lend, but they do want to help by providing essential items of furniture from their own stock, by buying household linen as a present, and by planting the allotment with delphiniums, scabious, larkspur and a hundred pink and white gladioli, to use for flower arrangements. So with Mary's and Michael's own contribution, careful costing and the staggering of purchases over a six-month period, the problem is solved to everybody's satisfaction. They could, of course, have asked their bank manager for an overdraft, but after all, they thought, a wedding is a family affair.

HOW TO SAVE UP AND RAISE MONEY

After a house and a car, a wedding is one of the largest items that a family is involved in financing. The amount can be substantial and it comes all at once out of an annual budget; a wedding is not something you can pay for on deferred terms through a mortgage or hire purchase.

Nevertheless, it is quite possible to make special plans for a wedding well in advance, in the same way as some parents plan to pay for school fees almost before their child is born; a proud father writes to a reputable financial newspaper for advice:

> 'I have three young daughters aged four years, two years, and one month. So that I will be able to cover the cost of weddings etc., as they arise in, say, 16 years' time, can you give me some idea of how much I should invest, in what, and for how long?'
>
> L. G., Milton Keynes

It is a matter of maximizing capital saved from income. But the problem is that, if it is the parents who are interested in doing the saving, they cannot know exactly when – if ever – the money will be needed, though the Office of Population Censuses and Surveys tells us that the average age for marrying is 24.1 years for men and 21.9 years for women.

Building societies offer a number of different schemes for planned investments, and some of them point out in their leaflets and posters the particular importance of planned saving for a wedding. Choices range from a simple deposit account at the lowest rate of interest, to subscription shares with twelve equal payments each year, to term-share arrangements suitable for people – like parents – who are after a high return over a fixed period. There are the new, highly competitive but limited issue, two-year capital bonds, which guarantee 1.75 per cent extra interest above the variable share account rate. There is a range of safe choices, and also the beginnings of variation and actual competition, among building societies, all of which can be affected by the money market in general and inflation in particular; if time has not run out, a careful check on what is available in a changeable situation is essential. And get hold of an independent comparative assessment if you can; the money pages in *Which?* do regular comparisons of rates. National Savings certificates need five years for the full advantage of the interest they offer to be felt; they are never a good choice for the non-tax payer, but a superb one for the higher tax payer. Endowment policies and friendly society plans with built-in tax and insurance advantages are possibilities for parents with longer vision, like the young father from Milton Keynes with three small daughters. And, they are a bonus if the girls turn out not to be the marrying sort.

Parents are likely to have saved up something for contingencies and emergencies, though not specifically for a wedding. Their contribution usually comes from a general pool of savings in one or more building societies, from savings certificates, granny bonds, Save-as-you-earn schemes or, like Daphne's father, from redundancy pay. When a family gets caught up in events beyond its control, it may be that savings have to be topped up with a loan. Bank managers are sympathetic to fathers with daughters, and to young couples, like Mary and Michael, with security and prospects. There are two possibilities to consider: a fixed, limited overdraft for a specified period, or a bank loan. If you want an overdraft, do not go ahead without asking first; the bank will not like it and may even refuse to pay your cheques. So discuss your needs and consider the conditions. You do not have to withdraw all the money you have asked for at once; you can take it out as you need it, and you pay interest only on the actual amount by which your account is in the red. On the other hand, you may have to pay out more in bank charges and you may have to provide some sort of security. If it is a loan you are after, you will find that there are two kinds: an ordinary bank loan and a personal loan. An ordinary loan is cheaper because you usually have, again, to provide security. With a personal loan, you do not have to provide security, but the original rates are fixed until you have paid off the loan.

You, or your parents, can also use the National Girobank personal loan scheme, which is available to anyone with a Giro account at the post office. They advertise loans for weddings in their advertising: relieved father, 'We can apply for a loan, love.' Reassured mother, 'Yes, and arrange it in time to make everything right for the day.' Quite a point here: make financial decisions and applications well in advance, so that the wedding is not spoilt by cares and concerns about whether you can afford it.

Credit cards enable you to get instant credit for a wide range of goods and services, and you do not need to have a bank account to get one. You simply

Although it is your day, it is often the little bridesmaids and pages who steal the show.

apply to the credit company of your choice and they send along a card if they consider you to be credit-worthy. Note that it is against the law for them to send you a card that you have not asked for. You can make repayments more or less when you like as long as you stick to the terms spelled out in your statement, which tells you the minimum amount you must pay. You can spread payments over a long period, but remember that the interest you pay is putting up the price of the things you have bought. And the rate can be over 23 per cent.

HOW TO DRAW UP A BUDGET

Budget. A dull, killjoy word, tainted with politics and dreary economies, not the kind of thing you want to associate with your wedding. Yet planning how to spend your money can bring you happiness based on security: the security of knowing where you stand and how far you can afford to deviate from your plans.

Normally, budgeting of the sort that you will need to consider when you are actually married falls into three categories: day-to-day spending, regular lump sums and occasional lump sums. You can work out the first two by keeping records for a trial period and checking up on old bills, receipts and cheque stubs. But the third is much more difficult because you do not have any previous patterns of spending to rely on. And there is the foreboding that everything will cost far more than you expected, and that you are bound to forget things you really ought to have thought about. Nevertheless, there are certain very definite steps you can take to help you plan your budget and your strategies for spending:

Work out exactly how much money you have coming in.

Set aside a quarter of this money for contingencies and all those things you will forget to take into account.

Write a list of all the goods and services you intend to buy and use.

Pick out those which are either unavoidable or fixed, like your marriage certificate.

Decide on your order of priorities.

Inquire and investigate: get guide prices for goods and several estimates for services so that you have a reasonable idea of the amount you might expect to spend.

Find out how the total of your proposed expenditure compares with your income.

Make any necessary adjustments and alterations.

Keep records and receipts, and check as you go that estimated and actual expenditure are roughly in line.

HOW TO CUT THE COSTS

The fact that over three million people are unemployed, has not curtailed wedding celebrations. Perhaps they are even more necessary. Circumstances may alter the celebrations, but they need not stop them being any the less joyful or memorable. Firstly, do things yourself wherever possible; you cannot avoid paying 15 per cent Value Added Tax (VAT) on most of the things you buy, but you do not have to pay out on services if you provide them yourself. (If you do choose to use a commercial service, find out whether the price you are quoted includes VAT, or specifically says 'All prices subject to VAT'.) There is little in a wedding that you cannot do for yourself, or find someone to help you with, if you really need to. D-I-Y not only saves money, but it means working together as a family and inviting friends to participate. Andrea's father made use of his contacts at the Rotary Club to get cake and cars, and her mother's friends at the Women's Institute coped with the catering.

Secondly, a wedding gives you the chance to learn new skills, to be experimental and creative: the local flower shop may not be so pleased, but it is quite possible to produce an acceptable buttonhole or corsage after practising with a piece of fuse or florists' wire and a few rosebuds from the garden; or better still, after going to flower arranging classes. You can turn any failures into fun, into a saga of do-you-remember when . . . the cake sank in the middle; Grandad's home-made wine blew the tops out of the bottles; and the cat licked the fish filling out of the flan. It is your attitude that counts, your intention to set your own standards and avoid comparisons with those other people sometimes attempt to impose.

Thirdly, you can be different, be unusual, be yourself; plan your wedding with spirit and panache – have an Edwardian picnic on the common, cheese and wine at the pub or an Oxfam lunch. Carry a bunch of your Dad's red dahlias or tiger-lilies. Choose a theme connected with one of your hobbies, especially one you happen to share, like cycling or sailing, horses or history: Elizabeth and John were keen on Roman history, so Liz wore her best yellow dress, which is the colour used in Roman marriages, with a veil half-covering her face and a wreath of myrtle and orange blossom. Sally and Simon gave up all their spare time to the local cricket club, and organized their wedding round a match, white flannels and striped blazers.

Finally, it is no sin to beg and borrow as long as you give things back cleaned and in good condition along with a personal note of thanks. People like to lend things for weddings, feeling part of the celebration, enjoying a kind of personal renewal of promises made long ago as they hand over veils, head-dresses and cake ornaments, as well as loaning cutlery and cake-stands. The old saying, 'Something old, something new, something *borrowed*, something blue' is still followed by many otherwise level-headed brides, who perhaps do not know that 'something blue' comes from a tradition in ancient Israel where the girl wore a blue ribbon as a symbol of purity, love and fidelity.

A SAVING SUMMARY

Get several quotations for any service you want to use, such as catering, photography or flowers, and look at them carefully, making sure you are comparing like with like. Check whether VAT is included.

Always read the small print on any document you have to sign. The smaller the print, the more care you need to take.

Borrow whatever you can – it is all part of the wedding tradition.

Plan your wedding as far in advance as you can; you get more choice and better value for money.

Work out your budget and keep tabs on everything you spend.

Look carefully at cancellation charges and deposits.

Spread the load and enjoy buying little by little over as long a period as possible; even going so far as to stock up your Mum's freezer with 'extras'.

Take stock of your skills and make the most of what you have got; learn new skills, like cake decoration or dress-making, or perhaps attend a specialist commercial course on organizing a wedding.

Make the most of friends who know how to do things; people love to be involved in weddings.

Enjoy being flamboyantly original or unusual.

HOW TO PLAN FOR PEACE OF MIND

Every bride has mishaps and misfortunes to talk about after her wedding that may not seem very funny at the time, but which somehow afterwards give personality and intensity to the memory. Do you remember when the page-boy stood on my train, when the best man dropped the ring down the central heating grid in the church, when the bridegroom got caught up in a traffic jam and the chief usher got his only set of car keys locked up in the boot? But much more serious disasters can and do happen both in the run-up period, in the form of illness and injury, and actually during the wedding in the form of theft, loss, food poisoning, and numerous other events concerning public or personal liability. Money cannot make up for a day spoiled, but it can bring you some compensation to offset extra costs at a time when you can least afford them. So it can pay you to consider insurance to give you peace of mind, and in some cases legal protection.

Though no company will insure you against a change of heart, you can get short-term cover in case your wedding has to be put off because of illness or accident. Remember that when you fill in any kind of proposal form, it is up to you to make a full disclosure of all relevant facts. Even if the company does not ask you the right questions, you have to provide them with what they might eventually consider the right answers. It is all very unfair. If, for example, your bridegroom is an enthusiastic pot–holer or polo player, and is injured in a final fling before the wedding, he will not be likely to get any compensation unless he has said on his proposal form that pot-holing or polo was his favourite sport.

You cannot insure against a rainy day, but if you are well prepared you will prevent it turning into a disaster.

Under more normal circumstances, an insurance company will want to know that you are both in good health and free from physical defect or deformity. Your premium will cover you for all expenditure that you would not be able to get back: church fees, deposits to car firms and photographers, cancellation fees to caterers. For a small extra sum, insurance can be extended to include 'postponement or cancellation of the wedding due to specified misfortune (death, accident, illness) overtaking the parents of the bride or groom'. Weather is a different matter: every bride wants the sun to shine on her wedding day, but. she cannot insure against rain, which brings discomfort and disappointment but not financial loss. A wedding is not like hospital, church or school fêtes, which are money-making events and can run at a loss because of bad weather. Your only protection here is to get your ushers to provide outsize umbrellas (ask golfing addicts) and laugh at your 'welly boot' wedding. At least you will get some good pictures.

You can also consider protecting your presents. Take reasonable precautions by asking a neighbour to sit in for you if you leave your presents at home while you are being married. Thieves are great opportunists, who read local newspapers to find out who is getting married, when, and where they live. See if you can get your parents' existing 'all risks' policy extended to cover theft on this special occasion – extension of an existing policy is always cheaper than setting up a new one. If you want to display your gifts at a hall or hotel, find out from the management if they already have an existing policy, or whether you yourself are expected to take responsibility. If you are, the same policy could be adapted to include the loss of your wedding or engagement ring.

Most families taking out ordinary house contents insurance are also covered for occupier's liability. This means that if the hanging basket you have planted with white begonias and trailing stephanotis tumbles down on the postman delivering your presents, compensation is available to him if he chooses to claim. Personal liability is built in too, so that you are covered for any damage you or your family cause to other people or their property, though it is usually limited to £250,000 plus legal costs. And you get employer's liability cover, which you might need if you pay someone to clean up or cater and she trips over that stone in the terrace that your Dad always intended to re-lay. It is always as well to tell the insurance company that there will be many more comings and goings than usual, particularly if you are having your reception at home.

If your reception is in a hotel, restaurant or hall, check with the manager about whose insurance covers responsibility for breakages and damage to furniture, fixtures and fittings. Weddings have been known to end in free fights before now, with the bride cowering under the table – and all because the guests were elbowing, jostling and competing with each other to get their pictures taken with the bride! Ask the manager if he has a public liability policy which would cover his kitchen staff or caterers in the event of an outbreak of food poisoning: at one wedding, the bride's grandmother died and a number of guests were taken seriously ill because of salmonella poisoning. Not a very likely event, however, and therefore one with a very low premium. You yourself might need a public liability policy if you are having a large wedding at home with a marquée on the lawn: ask the hirers if their men are covered by insurance while they are putting up and taking down the tent, if your guests are covered for injury caused, perhaps, by a pole or guide-rope breaking, and what happens if guests themselves cause damage either wantonly or accidentally. Get terms and conditions in writing at the beginning, so that you do not have acrimonious arguments after an unfortunate event. The chances are, of course, that none of this will happen, but it pays to be on the safe side.

TEN TIPS FOR SAVING MONEY

Take advantage of sales, particularly summer sales if you are going to want white shoes or sandals for a winter wedding. Even wedding dresses appear in sales, and Moss Bros sells off men's morning wear.

Take a look at chain stores for things like nighties and negligées or swimwear, especially in larger cities where there is a wider and sometimes experimental range of clothes.

Get married as late in the day as you can; tea parties come cheaper than traditional wedding breakfasts.

Have a home-made picnic on the lawn, village green or common.

Make the most of a local college that runs a catering course: can the students make and ice your cake, or even organize a buffet for you for not much more than the cost of the ingredients?

Get your publicity free: send in your own news to the free local press, and ask your photographer to send a photo.

Make your own invitation cards, place names, even Order of Service sheets, using pressed flowers and small silver bells and horseshoes carefully stuck on shiny white card. Write elegantly in black ink with a fountain pen.

Black cars can be cheaper than white ones of the same make, since they do double duty for funerals. With white satin ribbons and nylon net they look very elegant.

Think ahead and grow your own flowers from seeds, bulbs or corms. Ask the vicar if anyone else is getting married on the same day, so that you can perhaps arrange to share the cost of flowers for the church.

If you are having only a small number of guests, but would still like several tiers to your cake, consider using 'demonstration models' made of cardboard or styrofoam, iced and decorated, for one or more tiers.

2
PLANNING AND PREPARATION

PENNY went off to see what Australia was like. She not only liked it but fell in love with an Australian. Now she wants to come back to be married from her parents' home, in the little country church where she was christened. Yvonne went off to work in Newcastle, three hundred miles from her home, but she too wanted to come back for her wedding – even though she knew she could not arrive until the day before. Though more and more girls, like Penny and Yvonne, wander round the world and work away from home, six out of ten are still living at home at the time of their weddings. This makes organization much easier. But whether you are having a remote-control or a direct-contact wedding, its success depends on your attitude of mind; it is your approach that sets the scene, your tact, sensitivity and sound common sense, your flexibility that adapts to time, distance and circumstances. After all, you could organize a wedding in a week if you really had to. The important practical questions to keep on asking yourself are: 'What can we do with what we've got?'; 'Where do we go from where we are?'; rather than to work yourself into a state . . . 'If only we had more time, if only we lived nearer'. It is more likely, though, that it will be your mother who suffers from stress in the run up to the wedding. After all, responsibility does weigh heavily upon mothers, and they are the ones who remain behind when their daughters have departed amid a shower of flower petals and the clatter of old tin cans; they are the ones who cope with the chaos of clearing up, cake boxes and comments from neighbours. You are looking forward, she is looking back. Your wedding is an opportunity, perhaps for healing the breaches of the past, certainly for sharing a new experience, for working together, for creating a memory that will last a lifetime.

Opposite *This stylish and unusual dress, with its swirling skirt, is one that any bride would feel special in.*

COLLECTING THE FACTS

You cannot realistically plan, prepare and work out your priorities until you have got some hard facts to go on, to help you decide what you need and want, with your choice often depending on price, availability and timing. People try to rush you when they first see the sparkling ring on your finger. 'When's the wedding going to be, then?', 'Will you have a white dress?', 'What sort of a reception?' And it is very easy in your ecstasy to give instant answers and promises in all good faith, showering invitations on your friends in the office – promises which you may later find you cannot fulfil. So you are going to need not only general but also quite detailed information pretty early on to help you make your decisions and to forestall embarrassments.

When you start to plan your wedding, make a list of general headings, which will look something like this:

>ceremony
>reception
>transport
>wedding dress, accessories and clothes
>stationery and communications
>wedding cake
>flowers and decorations
>photography and filming
>other services & special requirements.

Your special requirements could include a wish – like Jane's – to have her class of nine-year-olds sing the twenty-third psalm she had so laboriously taught them; or – like Penny's – to have a military wedding with a guard of honour from the Australian army.

ASSESSING THE INFORMATION

To what extent can you rely on the information you collect? Certainly, everything the minister or superintendent registrar tells you will be beyond question, whether on organization, significance, legal and religious interpretation, or cost. But how knowledgeable are all those other people who overwhelm you with information and advice? Do they really know what they are talking about? Are their facts up-to-date, are they complete, or are you being told only the favourable aspects. When you choose the things that you need for your wedding, check that the information people give you is up-to-date and accurate.

It is more difficult to deal tactfully with family and friends, whose memories filter out unpleasant details, and for whom costs are firmly fixed in the past, than it is to deal with retailers and suppliers of services. After all, you do want to keep in touch with your family and friends ('Yes, Granny, I really will think about borrowing your warm wincey nightie for our holiday in Austria'), but you never need to see again the dress-shop assistant who told you how marvellous you looked when you felt like a pig's head on a platter with all those frills and flounces which you knew were just not your style.

You will also find magazines and specialist bride publications useful in giving you background information and a quick pointer to your needs and wants; you can spend a very happy evening flicking through current issues, finding out about goods and services and where to get them. You will also see a lot of advertisements designed to arouse your interest and attention and prod you into purchase. Advertisements fall into two clear groups, and a third not-so-clear group that is a mixture of the other two.

The first group – the kind you find in the *Yellow Pages*, in the small ads of your local newspaper, or at the end of bride magazines – give straight information: do you want a four-poster bed, a horse-drawn carriage, a flight of balloons with your names stencilled on to them, or do you want to know all about cakes and catering? You will find outline details of the product or service on offer, very often with an idea of the price range, and always with clear contact addresses and phone numbers so that you can easily get more information.

The second group do not deal so much with information as with persuasion, and for this reason they are likely to be full-page glossy pictures. The amount of print is small – apart from the words needed to draw your attention to a brand name – and if lists of suppliers and stockists are given, these are usually quite separate, on another page so that the photograph is free to make its impact. But you can use these pictures, the bulk of them being of wedding dresses, to give you an idea of the sort of thing you would like for yourself and how it looks with accessories chosen by an expert. Be aware, and appreciative, of the photographer's skills: he decides whether he wants a long shot, a mid shot or a close up. You will see plenty of close-ups of wedding rings on slender fingers: 'I bought her a ring to make her smile – and do you know, she just cried and cried and cried.'. The advertisement is a beautiful work of art, but it contains no useful information. Alternatively, photographers use a soft lens to give a gentle, romantic feeling to their pictures; they choose their camera angles carefully to show 'the product' in the most pleasing way, and they select backgrounds to catch the atmosphere of spring in the country or the serenity of an English summer.

However, many advertisements are a mixture of romance and realism, of information and persuasion. Just now and again, pause in your pleasure to underline the hard facts that you need to remember. You may eliminate most of the ad! And keep on reminding yourself that:

It is the natural function of an advertisement to sell you a product or a service, so it will not tell you about its drawbacks.

Magazines and specialist publications about weddings do not generally test the goods and services they recommend on a comprehensive basis, although they may try them out individually.

Articles and editorial comment are often based on information and press releases supplied by the manufacturer or retailer, on whom the magazines depend for income from advertising.

'*Happy bridesmaids make a happy bride.*'

The wedding industry, made up of large manufacturing or retailing chains, and countless small businesses often operating from home, is a good source of person-to-person advice, information and expertise. It is an industry that knows you are not likely to be a regular customer, yet it shows a great deal of care and concern, albeit commercial, for the people it serves. 'I knew I would never go back there', says Mandy, 'but they really made me feel special in that department store. The woman in the wedding boutique spent hours bringing out dress after dress even though she'd have to hang them all up again afterwards. She knew all about colours and shades of fabrics, and even advised me about make-up. And I wasn't charged any more for the dress being turned up. She told me to go back with the proper shoes.' The service industries you use have been through the same performance many times, but seldom show signs of staleness. This is your first appearance and you do need the support of experience: 'People drink too much if it's free,' says the manageress of a medium-sized hotel specializing in wedding receptions. 'Just have one glass of sherry per person set out on a silver tray, with soft drinks as well. I remember one reception where there was so much free drink that we had to put three of the guests to bed – free, of course.' It was this same manageress who could say with some conviction that, 'You can be pretty certain 10 per cent of the people you invite to your wedding won't be able to come.' Even though examples, experiences and expertise tumble out, value for money depends in the last resort on your own ability to explain what you want and to ask the right questions. Neither shops nor suppliers can help you unless you tell them your requirements. You can work out questions for each separate purpose by using basic question-words and phrases, such as, how? how much? how many? how do I pay? how long? when? why? who? where? what? what does it include?

BEING IN THE KNOW

As you build up background information you will come across nuggets of knowledge which will forever stand you in good stead. You will soon realize that your marriage contract is not the only one you are involved in making: every time you buy something, however small – a tube of glucose tablets from Boots to sustain you during the service – you are making a contract, even if you never say a single word. So your dress, shoes, veil, trousseau, cake, and flowers, are part of the normal contract that takes place every time you are involved in buying and selling. And this means that you, as one of the parties to the contract, can ask for special terms to be added when you are making your agreement. For example, it is especially important for things to be ready on time when a wedding is being organized. Take Joanne and Jim: they wanted to do everything just right, and they knew they ought to send out their printed invitations six weeks before the wedding. So they went to their local stationers twelve weeks in advance and ordered silver and white matching invitations, Order of Service sheets and compliments cards, deciding to pay half the money then to even things out even though it was more than the shop asked for as a deposit. The day came for them to collect their order. 'Sorry', said the girl thumbing through a pile of packets, 'they don't seem to be here. Perhaps they'll come in with the next batch.' So Joanne slipped into the shop in her lunch hour the following Monday. Still no cards. And there were no cards by the following Saturday, either. Joanne and Jim were beginning to get really anxious now. 'Let's try that little printer over the road. Perhaps he can do something quickly.' The printer said he could do simple invitations in black and white within a week, and he did. Then two weeks before the wedding, Joanne got a postcard from the stationers saying that her order was ready. She picked up the Order of Service sheets and the compliments cards, 'But I won't take the invitations, they're no use now. It's too late.' To her horror she was given an invoice that included the money outstanding for all three sets of cards. 'They're no use to us either with your names on,' said the manager, 'you'll have to pay.' And in tears Joanne did.

Any arguments about the rights and wrongs of this case could have been prevented if only Joanne and Jim had seen to it that words like 'time is of the essence' had been added in writing to the original order, with the deadline clearly spelt out. Flowers, cake, alterations to clothes, dry cleaning, shoe dyeing – any contract can be altered, and if the offer you make is accepted, you are on strong ground if something goes wrong. But if you do not make conditions before your offer has been accepted, you are bound to keep the goods or pay for the services. So, unless you ask in advance when you are buying your chain store nightie and negligée, 'Can I bring them back if he does not like strawberry pink with black spots?', you have no rights at all if they refuse to exchange them. Nevertheless, many shops as a matter of goodwill will let you change perfect goods that are the wrong size or colour, or even give you your money back, but they are not legally bound to do so.

Once you have made a contract you are required by law to. pay the full amount in cash: surprising in this day and age of cheques and credit cards. But the truth is that cheques and credit cards are a concession that a trader chooses to give you; of course, if he advertises that Visa, Access, American Express and so on are acceptable, then he has to stick to this part of the deal. So once again, before your offer is accepted, make sure that the method of payment is agreed quite clearly. Make sure, too, when you are ordering something in advance that you know what is going to happen if there is a delivery charge or a price increase. Check formal-looking contracts with special care – the smaller the print, the more critical you need to be in searching for phrases like 'subject to price fluctuation', or 'the price to be paid shall be that prevailing at the time of delivery'. You can always ask to take a contract away to look at before you sign it, and try to alter the points in it that you do not like. Or try somewhere else.

Look carefully at the question of deposits: it is entirely reasonable for a shop or supplier to want some sort of advance payment so they know that your intentions are genuine. Joanne and Jim were quite happy to pay a deposit on their stationery, and they were aware that it was a non–returnable deposit (since, as they later found out, their cards would not be any use to anyone else), to be used as part payment of their final bill. But Ian and Elise did not understand about their liability for cancellation fees: they went round looking at possible places for their reception and found three that they quite liked. Because of popular demand for peak Saturdays, they put down a 'deposit' of £20 on each. Then they found a superb Elizabethan barn with an ancient courtyard which would give a beautiful background for their photographs, and they set their hearts on this and started making all their plans. A month before the wedding, being a bit short of money, they went back to claim the refund of their original three 'deposits'. But the managers all assured them, pointing to the small print, that the deposit they had paid was also a cancellation fee. Perhaps if they had done something at an earlier stage the amount retained would have been less or possibly even waived entirely, but not with only a month to find a new set of customers.

Quotations and estimates provide the possibilities for other pitfalls. Sue rather vaguely asked a local car-hire firm for an estimate 'to transport herself and her family to the parish church and on to the reception' and was told £75. She accepted this and paid a third of it as a deposit. On her wedding morning the chauffeur presented Sue's mother with a bill on her way to church for £103.50 minus the £25 deposit. 'This isn't what we agreed.' 'No, but petrol's gone up in price, the journey was longer than we thought, and then of course there's VAT.' Sue's mother was furious, but she paid up, and did not argue because it was her daughter's wedding day. The problem was that Sue had not asked for a quotation, which is usually a fixed price for a specified job; whereas an estimate is only a general idea of the cost, which might even turn out to be less than expected. It is best to make the position quite clear by saying: 'Please give me a firm and fixed price for the job.'

PREFERENCES AND PRIORITIES

Having collected your information and classified it into your categories, you will now be horrified at the scale and scope of it all. 'Why don't we just elope?', wailed Sara. Perhaps you feel the same way in the face of this complex process of choosing, which not only confronts you and your fiancé, as one unit, but you and your mother as another, both interacting with two different families. But there are some preparations you can make which point the way to genuine consultation and diplomacy. You can try your hand at designing a preference chart, and then put all the results together so that you get an idea of the most popular choice. List, for example, all possible alternatives for your reception, ruling out any you know you cannot consider at all, and let each member of the family rank them in order of preference.

BRENDA'S PREFERENCE CHART

Heath Park Hydro Hotel	4
Village hall + outside caterer	1
Pig and Whistle	5
At home + caterer	2
At home D-I-Y	3

FINAL FAMILY PREFERENCE CHART

PLACE	Brenda	Philip	Mrs Sanderson	Mr Sanderson	Mrs McGeorge	Mr McGeorge	TOTAL	ORDER
Heath Park Hydro	4	5	4	5	1	5	24	4 =
Village hall + caterer	1	1	2	3	2	4	13	1
Pig and Whistle	5	4	5	4	5	1	24	4 =
At home + caterer	2	3	1	2	3	3	14	2
At home D-I-Y	3	2	3	1	4	2	15	3

A cool look for a summer wedding. The pink trimmings on the bride's dress match the pink of the bridesmaid's dress, and the same colour is used in the circlet of flowers that the bride is wearing, and in the bridesmaid's bouquet.

Brenda made it clear in advance that there would have to be fewer guests if they went to the hotel than if they chose any of the other places. You can see clearly from the chart that her mother-in-law, who still wanted to go to the Heath Park, and her father-in-law, who wanted to go to the Pig and Whistle, were equally out-voted. Brenda kept the peace by promising supplies of beer at the village hall and by inviting Philip's mother out for a shopping trip followed by lunch at the hotel. If you use this system, you may want to add brothers and sisters, or best man and bridesmaids to your list, or you might feel that the bride's and her mother's votes ought to count for more.

You will also find that there are certain things where your choice is quite clear cut, quite objective, depending on price, timing and availability of the size, colour, shape, model you happen to want. But there are others where the final choice is largely subjective, depending on taste, personal preference and on those inexplicable whims and fancies that we all like to indulge in. This is, however, the last stage in the choosing chain: it is no good letting yourself develop an attachment to a £250 satin crinoline wedding gown with a long train if you know you can only afford a maximum of £50, and need a dress you will be able to convert for evening wear. So how can you sort out your personal preferences, in an emotional situation where you perhaps feel ignorant and inexperienced. If your choice of style, shade and fabric has been narrowed down one way or another to eight possibilities, any of which you would be happy to wear, how can you make up your mind? It is your decision. You can try out the pairing system, which is made easier by the way in which wedding dresses are often identified by a name rather than by a style number:

Do you like	'Lucy' better than 'Louise'?	Yes	'Lucy'
	'Caroline' better than 'Sophie'?	Yes	'Sophie'
	'Hilary' better than 'Belle'?	No	'Belle'
	'Elvire' better than 'Blanche'?	Yes	'Elvire'
Do you like	'Lucy' better than 'Sophie'?	No	'Sophie'
	'Belle' better than 'Elvire'?	Yes	'Belle'
Do you like	'Sophie' better than 'Belle'	No	*Final result:* 'Belle'

You can use the same process for bouquets and cakes, head-dresses and veils, as well as for all those household items, such as curtains, carpets, chairs and cookers, that you will soon have to decide about.

DISCUSSING AND DECIDING

Now you are ready to face the family; the knowledge you have acquired will give you the confidence to cope with the problem of not being able to please everyone. Consultation and compromise are the key words. But the choice of date remains the bride's privilege – you are the one who names the day. Even here, though, there are constraints: you may find the vicar is booked up or has planned his holiday round a Bank Holiday. Or you may be like Martha and David. They are joint leaders of the local cub pack; not only do they intend to have their cubs in a guard of honour at the church, but they are going to camp with the cubs for their honeymoon. So in effect the availability of the county camp-site sets their wedding day for them. A new job, pressures at work, observance of Lent, even your own wish to take into account the finals of Father's football team or Grandad's local leek championship, can all interfere with your 'right' to choose, but any deviations must depend on you.

If you manage to steer clear of arguments over the actual allocation of money – who is paying for what – you may still give offence over the organization of guest lists. You are unlikely to run into problems with a small family wedding, but even here parents, grandparents, brothers and sisters, best man and bridesmaid can add up to quite a sizeable collection. But what if you set an upper limit of fifty guests? Do you divide this into twenty-five for each family? Fair on the face of it, but what if the groom is the youngest of six with all his brothers and sisters already married, most of them with children? Resentments remain and affect relationships: Margaret, intending to support a student husband, was paying for her own wedding, but her mother-in-law kept on inviting her own friends and neighbours to the wedding without any consultation. Months later, faced with an overdraft that never got smaller, Margaret was still bitter. Technically and traditionally it is your mother's job to compile the guest list, in consultation with the groom's family, but in Margaret's case she did not have a mother to help her cope with a situation which was beyond her.

It is a good idea at an early stage to make a list of people you would like to invite, those your fiancé would like, and those the parents would like – in addition to the agreed essentials. This is the area where there may have to be bargaining and trading off, perhaps brutally, depending on who is paying the bill. However, you could consider altering the place to suit an agreed policy of entertaining the greatest number of people at the lowest possible cost. In Brenda's case, all the guests that everyone wanted could be invited, if they changed to an outside caterer at home. After all, this was the corporate second choice, including Brenda's, Philip's third (and all he really wanted was for Brenda to be happy) and, most important of all, Mrs Sanderson's first choice.

The other difficult subject is babies and young children. You have to bear in mind that if you exile young children, you may also be excluding your best friends who cannot get baby-sitters. Could you put up with a bawling infant drowning your solemn promises, or an insuppressible toddler tired of his toy train shouting out during the minister's address? You can gamble, and find to your surprise that the most turbulent child is totally awed into silence by ceremony and circumstance, and does nothing worse than wipe his nose on your long veil. But if you cannot organize a crèche at the home of a friend or neighbour, you must word your letters of explanation and rejection with the utmost tact – even your nearest and dearest are touchy about their children. The actual invitation will of course be addressed to Mr and Mrs B. A. Quiverful. And your decision has to be all or nothing: you cannot invite little Gareth because he is always as good as gold and at the same time exclude young Tom, who is known to be a real tearaway. Being selective will cause long-term ill feeling; a fair and firm ruling might not cause more than instant irritation.

PLANNING AND PARTICIPATING

You are in a much more positive position when you start talking about participation – who wants to do what and when – because people like to be actively involved in your preparations. It can be helpful to draw up job cards – plain post or index cards will do – reminding people of what they have agreed to do and what they need to know: it is no use Brenda taking advantage of her in-laws offer to take back the hired wine glasses the day after the wedding if they do not know the name of the shop, the details of deposit paid, and rules about breakages.

Even traditional 'jobs' can be itemized, and presented in duplicate to a forgetful father:

12.15   Leave with the bride (that's me) for St Mary's.
         Check you've got your house key, and remember
         black shoe polish doesn't come off white dresses.
         Watch your feet.

12.30   Escort the bride into church, and walk up the
         aisle with her on your left – the vicar will give
         you the sign.
         Give her away. The vicar will tell you when.
         You don't say anything, just take my hand palm
         downwards. Then sit down next to Mum.
         Get to the hotel first with Mum and Bill's parents
         to receive the guests.
         Make your speech when we have cut the cake,
         and don't say anything embarrassing like alleging
         that Bill doesn't know one end of a dishcloth
         from the other!

The people with the longest job lists of all are you and your mother. You cannot always conform to a countdown, but you can set out all the tasks you have to do and then put them in an order which suits you:

Make arrangements with the minister or superintendant registrar and decide on a date and time.

Decide on your style of reception, and make any necessary bookings with halls, hotels and caterers.

Work out your provisional guest list, consulting both families.

Choose your bridesmaids and get your bridegroom to choose his best man. Who do you want for ushers?

Consider your colour schemes and themes, and discuss these with your bridesmaids.

Look at different types and styles of wedding cake and order yours.

Order your stationery: invitations, compliments cards, Order of Service sheets, cake boxes, and any extras such as monogrammed napkins, drink mats or matchboxes.

Book your photographer, deciding whether you want him at home first as well as at the ceremony, reception and departure.

Consider your clothes, and then buy your wedding dress and accessories, your going-away outfit and your honeymoon requirements. Look at them as a whole, not as separate items.

Buy your wedding ring. Maybe you are having one each?

Order your 'official' cars and work out who is going to need help with transport from friends and relations.

Find a bouquet to fit your style of wedding, and order this together with buttonholes and corsages. Decide on flower arrangements for both ceremony and reception.

Send out your invitations about six weeks before your wedding, together with a sketch map showing how to get there and where to park.

Decide how you can tactfully tell people what you would really like for a present. Are you going to circulate a list, place one with a shop, or ask your mother to deal with it all?

Make up your mind about the music, discuss it with the minister and the organist. Would you like a choir, a string quartet, a peal of bells?

Confirm your decisions about menus and wines with your hotel or caterer – or your mother – and tot up your final number of guests.

Make an appointment at your hairdressers for your wedding day, early in the morning, discussing your special requirements well in advance.

Send in your press announcements, checking up on timing as there can be a surprisingly long time-lag.

Check that your bridegroom has done something about gifts for the bridesmaids. He will need reminding about this.

Make discrete inquiries about his clothes, particularly that old rag of a cricket club tie that he might just be going to wear.

Plan for peace of mind, and have a rehearsal so that everyone knows who is doing what. Do not be superstitious, though.

Opposite *'It's the most important day in your life; it's a ceremony to remember for ever and ever.'*

Your countdown may be frighteningly condensed: Yvonne – as her diary shows – only had three months, but she still coped by remote-control from Newcastle.

April 30th   Bill and I choose the date – August 9th – or rather it chooses us because our holiday is already fixed and the car booked on the midnight crossing to Calais.

May 1st   Mum sees the vicars for us. Two of them, because the one in our parish will be away in August. He is going to get in touch with his friend at St Mary's.

May 2nd   The date is confirmed, but we have to find out about special licences. How *do* you write to an Archbishop?

May 3rd   I must write to ask my young sister to be my bridesmaid. She is in Singapore just now, so I will tell her to get a dress made. Yellow silk chiffon, I think, because yellow and white will be our colours.

May 9th   Mum finds out about receptions. Difficult in summer; but she gets a cancellation at The Mill, which is what we wanted most. We will go and see Bill's parents today and ask them about guests. Bill's Dad has a dominoes match on August 9th!

May 1st

Dearest Yvonne,

I have succeeded in making arrangements for you to be married off! I've arranged with the Vicar of St Mary's that he will dispose of you at 12.30 on August 9th – just as you wanted. When you've chosen your invitations, the wording should be: Watford Parish Church (St Mary's).

You will obviously need a special licence, as you don't live at home any more, and I've been given details as to how to get one from the Archbishop of Canterbury's legal secretary. I will write to him today.

The Vicar of St Mary's is very nice and helpful and wants to see you both next time you come for a weekend.

I have also been to the local college to talk about making you a wedding cake. We agreed that the students wouldn't buy a decoration for the top tier – that vase off our cake that you wanted would look best with small fresh flowers.

Much love,
Mum.

June 28th

Dearest Bill,

I am writing to you because I don't know when Yvonne is intending to move out of her flat and into the new house. Where she is right now, I've no idea! I enclose a letter from Michael and me giving our consent to your marriage. Even though you are both over twenty-one you will need this, with one from your parents and another from the Vicar of St Mary's, when you apply for your special licence.

I went to The Mill again yesterday and settled for the buffet menu you chose (avoiding the black forest gâteau). You can have wine on a sale-or-return basis, so there's no need for us to decide now on the number of bottles. The Manager suggested you might like to consider their house wine instead of the Graves and the Beaujolais. What do you think? They'll serve sherry before lunch, and there'll be Newcastle Brown Ale as well as plenty of soft drinks.

I can't do anything for another week about photographers or cars, because I'm going to be away until next weekend. But first I need to know about your parents. Do I assume they won't need a car because someone will have brought them direct to St Mary's from Newcastle? And what about your best man? – will he be taking you to the church in his car?

See you next weekend. Your appointment with the Vicar is at 6.30 on Saturday, and the organist says you can call in on him afterwards to discuss your music.

With love,
Alma.

KEEPING RECORDS

Diaries, details of day-to-day planning and organization, these are things that you can hand on to history. Do you know that in the 1950s you could get a beautiful broderie anglaise wedding gown for under £20, a lace-trimmed veil for £3.50, a honeymoon nightie for £1.50? That it was quite usual to find coal buckets, toasting forks and fire-side sets on wedding-present lists? But making history is not your immediate concern, though in years to come you will smile happily as your children and grandchildren think, how interesting, how quaint. The real point in keeping records is, firstly, to help you see at a glance where you are on your schedule, what still needs to be done, what needs to be checked, and how the money is going; and secondly, to provide you with evidence in writing of every decision reached, every letter written, every agreement signed. It is fine to use the telephone for your first inquiries and final check-ups, but any crucial arrangements concerning dates and times, numbers and money, must be confirmed in writing. It is no good trusting to memory in an argument. For the same reason, keep every invoice, receipt, price tag, Post Office counterfoil, cheque or credit card stub: difficult-to-file, but nevertheless essential, clutter. For that reason, you may find it better to work out your own system for collecting and classifying, rather than to buy a special bride's record book; a special book may look more glamorous, but your own version can turn out to be more practical and more personal. You might consider an A4 loose-leaf file supplemented by a cardboard folder for all those non-standard bits and pieces it is so important to keep. You will obviously want to include the following items in your record:

Details of your budget and how your spending is in line with your estimates.

Your time-table of events.

Your list of who is doing what and when, with addresses and telephone numbers.

Your guest list.

Your wedding-present list with details about who gave you what and when you acknowledged it.

Your final check-list.

Your plan for the day, remembering to allow about five hours if you are having your hair done, from breakfast in bed to final departure.

A check-list of things that need to be done while you are away, from coping with the cake to caring for your cat.

You may need to turn some of these items into tables where you can put ticks and crosses and convenient comments. Belinda developed her guest list into something much more comprehensive:

NAME	DATE OF INVITATION	YES/NO	ANY SPECIAL NEEDS	CAKE
Mr & Mrs Sellars	June 15	2	—	—
Mr & Mrs White	June 16	2	1 diabetic.	—
Mr & Mrs Dunlop	June 16	0	—	✓
Mr & Mrs Evans	June 16	2	New set of false teeth!	—
Misses Fuller	June 17	2	Overnight accommodation, and transport to church.	—

You may turn out to be consumed by collecting, and find that functional record-keeping turns into the creation of a souvenir, the making of a memory, with samples of your wedding invitation, your menu, samples of dress materials, press announcements. What you do is up to you.

3
CHOOSING AND CHECKING

Do you remember chanting old skipping rhymes when you were a little girl? If you tripped over the twirling rope you were 'out'; this was childhood's way of choosing. When will it be? This year, next year, sometime, never. What will you wear? Silk, satin, muslin, rags. Where will it be? How will you get there? The thudding feet in the playground beat out the message that life is all a matter of luck and extremes, that decisions are made by destiny. But you can determine your own destiny by being conscious that choice often does exist, that it is you yourself who can control and shape the final reality. However, restrictions and regulations exist and you have to fight your way through these, accepting some, rejecting others, consulting and compromising; and finally creating. In other words, if you cannot have exactly what you want, how do you turn a second-best option into a first-rate wedding?

CHURCH, CHAPEL, CATHEDRAL . . .?

Susan had to face this problem. As a child, she had sung in the choir at her local church, where weddings took place nearly every Saturday. 'Praise my soul, the King of Heaven' was her favourite hymn. One day, she dreamed, she too would walk up this long familiar aisle with its old, frayed red carpet. One day another choir would sing that hymn for her. But the dream was not to be. Now, ten years later, Susan was in tears because she could not be married in the church of her choice. Why not?

She did not live in the parish, nor did she worship at the church any longer since she now worked out of the area. The present vicar, as is his moral right, was adamant that he would not marry couples who did not show a serious, regular commitment to his church. So Susan had to shop around for a vicar to perform her ceremony, for vicars, too, come in all shapes and sizes and vary in attitude and interpretation. The second vicar, though willing and full of wise counsel, comfort and consolation, was going to be away on holiday. The third was not only available, but he was also someone with whom she had an instant rapport. So Susan's wedding day was not a childhood dream fulfilled, but neither was it a substitute, or second best. It was something she herself had suffered for and striven for. It was her day.

YOUR RIGHT TO CHOOSE

Provided you are of age, are legally free to marry, and recognize the law's basic requirement that 'notice shall be given' of your intent, where do your 'rights' exist? In most cases, you can decide whether you want a religious or a civil ceremony, and this is the one choice where money must not influence your decision; in any case, the essentials for either service amount to very little. Most first-time brides, however, do seem to prefer a religious ceremony because it offers so much more than the brief civil contractual commitment in a register office, which often cannot accommodate all the guests they want to invite, even though technically the marriage must take place 'with open doors'. Though registrars do their best with décor and flowers, they cannot offer the atmosphere, the traditions, the wider symbolism and the age-old rituals that a religious ceremony gives even to those who are not normally devout. Nevertheless, some brides do deliberately choose a register office because they would feel hypocritical about 'using' a church when it suited them; in any case, even for early Christians marriage was a secular and not a religious affair.

Other brides, because of divorce or a difference of religion, have no choice at all. But no one can take away from them their freedom to organize whatever sort of service they want once the law has been complied with. Ministers will devise blessing ceremonies in church, or couples can work out their own form of service, to be held wherever they want: Sandra and Eric chose the grounds of a ruined abbey, Anne and Gareth a beach in the moonlight, Margaret and Tom a rough wooden shelter on a mountain top where the winter wind whipped away the pages of John Donne's seventeenth century poem: 'I wonder, by my troth, what thou and I did till we loved?'

The fact remains, however, that in Britain – unless you are Jewish, or mortally ill and need a last-minute ceremony in hospital – you cannot get married in an unregistered building, which leaves you with just two choices. In some countries you can get married in all sorts of peculiar places – under water, in the air, on snow or ice. You might not want this particular freedom, but still hanker after a reasonable third choice of being able to get married at home, in the garden or even in the local park with a civil marriage celebrant carrying out the service. There is a strong case for an acceptable third alternative, which countries such as Australia and the USA now offer.

As a bride, you are the one who traditionally has the right to name the day. But your choice is subject to availability and opening hours just like any other public or commercial service. The date and time you want, particularly during the summer, may have been booked up long since; or you may find yourself crammed in and queuing up in a production line at the church door or register office threshold. Do not take advantage of a bride's privilege to be late or you may miss your moment. On the other hand, do not be too early; be prepared to cruise round in your car, or you may find yourself matched to the wrong man.

There are other constraints – legal constraints – that you have to check up on, whenever and wherever you decide to get married. If you choose a register office wedding and want to get married the cheapest way, that is, by Certificate, one of you will have to live in that area for seven days before you go in person to tell the registrar that you would like to get married. Then you allow twenty-one clear days between the day when you see him and your wedding day. You can cut down time but increase the cost, which still remains very modest, and get married by Licence. This time you must live in the area for fifteen days, but then you need only one clear day before you can get married. Your Certificate or Licence will remain valid for three months.

If, on the other hand, you want to get married in the Church of England, you will have to stick to similar timing regulations; these rules will also allow you to be married either in the parish where you or your fiancé lives, or in the church you usually go to – provided that you are on the electoral roll in that parish. Susan could not be married where she wanted because neither of them fulfilled any of these qualifications.

So circumstances as well as choice push you towards four possibilities: getting married after the publication of banns, by common Licence or Superintendent Registrar's Certificate, or by Special Licence. Most girls are still living at home with their parents when they get married, so they are more likely to choose the tradition of calling the banns on three consecutive Sundays. This public declaration of intent – and the possibility of being 'banned' or prevented from being married – goes back to the seventeenth century, when the Puritans saw the Anglican Book of Common Prayer as popish. So they brought in a form of civil marriage in which couples wanting to get married had to inform the parish registrar, who then called the banns on three separate occasions. The important point was that these occasions should be public, so banns were called not only in church but in the market-place on market day amidst the cows and goats and chickens. A Licence, however, got rid of the need to have banns called, and though parents paid a higher price to get one, they saved money in the long run by not having to provide festivities for a public wedding. For us, marriage by banns is still the cheapest way: the more you digress from this system, the more you pay – paying progressively for your privacy and protection from publicity, and for your freedom to choose time and place. The Special Licence from the Archbishop's Registrar is by far the most expensive form of exemption: including exemption from the normal opening hours of 8 am until 6 pm.

CHECK-LIST FOR YOUR CEREMONY

Have you got the correct name and address of the place where you are going to be married? In some towns there may be three or four churches all dedicated to St Andrew – make sure you get the right one. Your minister will tell you, or the registrar will have an up-to-date list of all registered places of worship.

Which service do you prefer? You have three choices here. The most ancient version is the Book of Common Prayer of 1662 where you have to promise to obey your husband. The 1928 modified version, largely chosen by Princess Diana, leaves out obedience. The Alternative Service Book of 1980 leaves obedience up to you and offers a selection of prayers for you to choose from.

Where do you want to sign the register? May you sign it publicly in front of the congregation if you wish, or privately in the vestry?

How do you want to make your vows? Do you want to repeat short phrases after the minister, or would you rather learn them off by heart and perhaps then stand facing each other so that your family and friends can see more and hear better?

Have you any special requests? Beth wanted her young brother to sing 'I'll walk beside you'; Theresa wanted the two fathers to read a lesson each; Barbara wanted her great-grandmother, who was in a wheelchair and also very deaf, to be placed where she could hear and see.

Who will actually solemnize your marriage? The answer is: any clerk in holy orders from a bishop to a curate. But what if your favourite uncle is Canon at the local cathedral? You may ask the minister if Uncle Donald can perform the ceremony, but it would be a courtesy to invite the minister to take some part in the service.

What sort of music? Must it be religious or can it be modestly secular? Is there a choir? If not, may you consider other possibilities? Are bell-ringers available?

May photographs be taken inside the church? Are they acceptable if flash is not used? Are there any restrictions in the vestry?

Are video recordings of the ceremony allowed? If not, may you tape record your vows at the rehearsal?

May you choose your own colour schemes and styles for flower arrangements? Are there any restrictions during church festivals such as Lent or Advent?

May guests throw confetti as you come out of church? Is there an extra charge for this (for sweeping up later)? If not, are there acceptable alternatives such as rice, wild bird food, or fresh flower petals? Check up on local litter laws; if a church door opens directly on to the street, your guests will not be able to throw confetti.

What style of dress? Maybe you are planning to wear an off-the-shoulder dress. Will this cause offence – even if you wear a long veil with it?

How much will it all cost? When is it best to pay? The cost of banns and certificate are fixed by the Church Commissioners, but charges for verger, organist, choir, bell-ringers, and additional items like red carpets and awnings outside, vary according to the parish and the vicar. Since the vicar puts in so much effort and receives no direct payment in return, you might like to consider a special personal donation to his church. Some vicars stipulate that a collection is taken; occasionally hinting to guests that they should relate their gift to the value they put upon their own marriage. It is a good idea to pay the church fees when you go for your rehearsal, unless you can rely on the best man to deal with the fees immediately after the ceremony.

'With this ring . . .'

'AND SHE SHALL HAVE MUSIC'

Where was Wanda? She had set off with her father for the village church, in the pony-trap that a farmer friend had lent for her wedding day. Soon the pony's steps became very irregular and he hung his head. He had lost a shoe. Wanda hopped out and hitched the horse to a lamppost while Dad popped into the local garage where the boss got a car down from the ramp and drove Wanda off to her wedding – twenty minutes late. In the meantime what was happening at the church? The organist had played Bach's 'Sheep may safely graze' and his routine repertoire twice through, followed by a suitably muted medley of Beatles' music; and now the vicar was rehearsing the congregation in 'O love divine', moving on to the end of the last verse with a final triumphant 'Amen' as the bride arrived.

Music can be a significant part of a church wedding, but not normally as significant as it was in Wanda's case. It is an integral part of the service – and it is you who control its integration. It can contribute to the atmosphere that you want to create, separating and marking the different stages of your ceremony, emphasizing the various moods. It is part of you, part of your familiar past yet pointing to an unknown future; it also belongs to the Church and therefore envelops you in something greater than yourself; it is tied in with ritual and festival that are already age-old.

Your choice of music should not be left to the last minute. In any case, for purely practical reasons, you will need to make your decisions – and these are essentially shared decisions – early on: if you are having Order of Service sheets, you will want to have these printed along with the rest of your stationery about three months before your wedding. Possibilities and practicalities should be discussed with minister and organist before you come to any firm conclusions. And there are little matters of copyright to be considered. A small acknowledgment may be enough; if a hefty fee is payable, you might want to change your mind.

The formality and framework of the wedding service determine the occasions when music is appropriate, although you do not have to use music at all if that is your choice. But most brides want music, usually organ music, though they may have to put up with a Sunday school piano, supplemented by congregation and choir. The choice of music is wide ranging, and the particular parts of the ceremony that you need it for are:

To fill in the time before your arrival, and to set the scene.

To herald your arrival and to accompany you as you make your way down the aisle on your father's arm.

To occupy and interest the congregation while you are signing the register, and tidying yourself up.

To enable your family and friends to take an active part in celebrating your marriage.

'IF MUSIC BE THE FOOD OF LOVE'

Specialist guidance from the minister, organist and choirmaster are essential even if you are both great music lovers: you are not likely to have heard public performances in the church, which may have peculiar resonances, and you cannot know the capabilities of a creaking noisy old organ.

Shared preferences are important: the associations you have built up together, the hymns you learnt long ago at school or shared with friends at their weddings, the music your parents chose, the theme music from a favourite TV programme like 'Nunc dimittis' – 'Now dismiss us' – from *Smiley's People*, or even a half-remembered childhood blessing like 'God be in my head and in my understanding'.

Tradition may influence you, so that you look no further than Mendelssohn's 'Wedding March' from *A Midsummer Night's Dream*. Timing will affect your choice; you will need to match your entrance music to the length of the aisle, for example, and you will need something that you can walk gracefully in time to.

Availability of sheet music and appropriate performing rights will determine whether or not you can indulge in a more unusual choice.

It is important for people to participate in the service, to sing hymns, and psalms like 'The Lord is my shepherd', and 'I will lift up mine eyes unto the hills', which are familiar to them. You will probably want three hymns: one to be sung when you arrive and stand before the chancel steps, another after the marriage ceremony, and another after the Blessing. Take a look in a hymn-book at both wedding hymns and your own favourites in the general section, like 'Lead us, heavenly Father, lead us'.

You might want to fit in with a particular church festival, such as Christmas, Easter or harvest time, using seasonal hymns and background music.

'THEY WERE MY CHOSEN MUSIC'

Sadly, no wedding bells for Wanda because she was being married during the peak of the summer and the bell-ringers were all away on holiday. She had chosen 'Sheep may safely graze' to set the scene for her country wedding, but because of the mishap with the trap she also got the Beatles, which she had not bargained for. She walked down the aisle accompanied by 'Fanfare for a Bride' by Sir Arthur Bliss which gave her time to get her breath back before the first hymn; not a wedding hymn but an old school hymn, 'The King of Love my shepherd is', which followed 'Sheep may safely graze'. Her second hymn was the well-practised 'O love divine' sung with exceptional vigour, and the choir sang 'Jubilate Deo in C', which was written at the request of the Duke of Edinburgh for the choir of St George's chapel, while the register was being signed. The final hymn? 'Praise my soul', chosen because it was a family custom, followed by

Widor's 'Toccata' from 'Symphony No. 6' as a triumphant finale as Wanda and her husband moved slowly from the dimness of the church into the bright summer sun.

'SWEET SINGING IN THE CHOIR'

You may have set your heart on the soulful singing of small boys in white surplices and well-starched ruffs. But again this is a service which is subject to availability: children will be at school for weddings during the week and you may have to make do with the best efforts of local pensioners. And even the most devoted choirboy is going to chafe in the summer at the continual constraints on his free time on Saturdays. Choirs – like bell-ringers – tend to disband in August, so you may have to think of an alternative style of choral music – a friend or young brother to sing 'I'll walk beside you', or a madrigal group to do an arrangement of 'Greensleeves'. Or change tactics and bring in a harpist, a trumpeteer to play a real trumpet voluntary, or a string quartet.

You do have to bear in mind that choirboys – and girls – are quite realistic about weddings, which they see as a pleasant way of topping up pocket-money. They may look angelic, but even the best of them have to be reminded 'never to talk or whisper or eat sweets during service' and to sit straight: 'Do not cross your legs, be careful your cassock always covers them – trousers or bare knees do not look well in the choirstalls.' Try the choir out at morning or evensong, perhaps when you go to hear your banns being called. But remember, you cannot expect them to appreciate the special significance of your ceremony. 'When I was nine', said Wanda's husband after their wedding, 'I used to knock up a nice little income as a choirboy. I often wondered what couples could possibly see in each other, and about the strange looks they gave each other. I used to wink knowingly at Mark. But I didn't really know. Today at last I understand what it's all about.'

CELEBRATION

Helena had her reception in a hotel car park. She did not want to greet her guests on a forbidding slab of black tarmac, but she had no choice. Her only choice, in fact, was to make what she could out of a difficult situation. What had happened? She had booked the hotel ten months before her wedding with all the arrangements confirmed in writing, and a month beforehand she had agreed her menu with the manager. But a last minute check-up produced the shame-faced admission that there was another wedding – same day, same time, same place. The hotel had double-booked, and Helena was the one they had chosen to be the victim of their incompetence. So what was she to do with 150 guests and no reception? She persuaded the manager to put up a marquee in the car park and to set aside one of the downstairs bars, and decided to be defiantly original as well as essentially practical: in order to avoid the clash of coinciding brides at the hotel, she would have her cake-cutting ceremony and speeches *first*. So, straight after the wedding service friends and onlookers were invited into the adjoining school hall for tea and cake. Helena did not let disappointment, despair or even rightful resentment spoil the occasion. But her parents were far from pleased when they later received a bill for the normal price; they deducted £100, sent it to the vicar and decided to let the matter drop. After all, they did not want to spoil their daughter's wedding by complaining!

WHERE WILL IT BE?

Your reception is the most costly item in your wedding budget, but it is also the most controllable. In Elizabethan times, it was the custom for parents to hold a party or bride-ale which anyone could go to by paying an admission charge. Sometimes these celebrations became extremely rowdy, and by-laws were brought in to restrict the amount of beer that could be brewed and to limit the number of 'guests' to thirty-two.

Helena could have chosen her own home or a hired hall, a pub or a club; and in retrospect she might have preferred any one of these to what she finally got. So

This is a popular choice of outfit for pages. However, there are many alternatives, so have a look around. If you look at old paintings and book illustrations, you may come up with some designs of your own.

why did she want a hotel reception in the first place? She had to accept that both she and her mother would be working right until the week before the wedding, so they needed someone with experience to take overall responsibility. They wanted predictable outgoings so that they could know exactly how much everything would cost, with no hidden extras. They were aware they would need to take into account the comfort and convenience of guests whose ages ranged from eight to eighty-eight, and to have the use of facilities like a changing room for the bride.

Why this particular hotel? Two of her friends had lovely receptions there in delightful surroundings, with just the right sort of romantic atmosphere. She and Simon had, moreover, enjoyed a candlelight dinner there when they got engaged. The hotel was experienced in organizing conferences, banquets and weddings, and it appeared in the good food guides that Helena had consulted. It was central, easy to find, with large lawns and flower gardens – and a large car park!

PLACES: THEIR PROS AND CONS

	ADVANTAGES	DISADVANTAGES
HOTEL	Less work; delegation of responsibility; predictable prices; range of menus–choice and price; general comfort and provision of facilities; car parking; ancillary services such as overnight accommodation; possibility of arranging a dance or disco.	Likely to be the most expensive choice; numbers may be limited; possibly impersonal–a mass-produced production line wedding; need to book well in advance; times may be restricted particularly on Saturdays–perhaps a rival function; VAT to be paid.
HALL	Can accommodate large numbers of people; gives choice of **buffet or sit-down meal;** freedom to do what *you* want; probably has car park; cheap; disco or dance possible; part of the local community.	Often bare and functional; limited catering facilities; doubtful heating; shortage of electric points; need to hire equipment; problem of matching the caterers with the facilities; poor cloakrooms; clearing up the crumbs afterwards.
HOME	Personal, intimate, friendly–the 'right' place; you can do what you like when you like; timing is more flexible; cheap–unpaid labour and no VAT.	Numbers generally limited; a tendency to crowd and cram; a load of hard work at a stressful time; organization down to the last detail; clearing up afterwards; inadequate toilet and cloakroom facilities; no one to blame if things go wrong.

UNUSUAL RECEPTIONS

Since you have only two choices for your ceremony, you might want to be deliberately unorthodox in your place and style of reception. But originality can be risky–just think of the bride who booked Cardiff castle for her reception, and then found herself surrounded and serenaded by thousands of pop fans who had come for a concert in the grounds, which had been hired separately for the same day. If you cram yourself into an old railway carriage, you may find that competent catering and circulation among your guests is impossible; a binge in a boat off Brighton pier may make everyone ill; that a rooftop garden cannot provide shelter in a sudden summer downpour. So you do need time to check up on details, and a good deal of imagination to foresee and forestall problems. Even with an apparently predictable place, Helena's imagination was incapable of conjuring up a car-park wedding; but the fact that, in her particular case, choosing and checking did not turn out well, does not invalidate the general principle: that it is *always* a good idea to have a list of things to do and find out. In any case, many of her points were perfectly adequately covered.

HELENA'S CHECK-LIST FOR THE HOTEL

Find out if the date and time I want are available, connecting up with the arrangements we have made for the wedding service. Is the hotel going to be free for us to use in the evening?

Check whether they can cope with a hundred and fifty guests, ten of them children – I think they would like a table to themselves.

Look at the range of set menus and their prices for both sit-down and buffet meals; do not let them take me in with any special jargon – I am not really sure at the moment about the difference between a fork and a finger buffet. Can I alter any of their menus to suit myself? I cannot stand Black Forest gâteau and I'd much rather have fruit salad.

Talk about wine. I do not really know very much about it, so I need extra help here. Perhaps they have an all–in wine package, which would make it easier for us to know the exact cost for each guest. If they do not do this, must I supply my own and is there a corkage charge? Or do they supply on a sale-or-return basis? Maybe they have some good house wines like that red in a carafe that Simon and I had when we got engaged. I suppose they must have a licence, but does it need to be extended if our disco goes on until late? And I think we really ought to have a pay-bar during the evening.

Discuss financial arrangements. What is their practice for deposits, cancellation fees and stages of payment? Is there an overall price so that we can work out the exact cost for each guest? Is VAT automatically included? And is there a service charge? Are we expected to tip anybody? And what about insurance cover, not just for liability, but for the presents that we would like to show off?

Work out the time schedule: when do they need to know about numbers – both a rough idea and the final facts? When do we decide on seating arrangements and the timing of speeches? And when will they want our cake delivered – and do they have a silver stand to put it on and a knife with a white satin ribbon?

Find out about flowers. Do they arrange for central displays in the entrance hall? And what about small posies on the tables? I would really like to be able to have pink and white tea-roses from my grandparents' garden. Can we do this? How much do the various alternatives – and I need to know what these are – cost? I want to have a planned colour scheme, with deep-pink napkins and candles on a white starched cloth to link up with the roses.

Take a look at the cloakrooms and toilet facilities. Will I have to pay to have someone on duty? Look at the car park; see if there are any steep steps that my grannie could not get up. Can we have chairs and little tables out on the lawn if it is fine?

Ask if there are two rooms where we can get changed afterwards, and whether there are special terms for people who need to stay overnight.

Get all of this confirmed in writing.

FOOD FOR THOUGHT – HELENA'S MENUS

She contemplated a range of some dozen hot 'sit-down' menus, which started off appetizingly humble:

Green pea soup
Grilled gammon with fried egg
Baked potato   Garden peas
Fresh fruit salad and ice cream
Coffee

and moved up-market into French classical cuisine with:

Smoked salmon cornets with prawns
Consommé aux Madeira paillettes d'or
Tournedos Rossini
Pommes Lyonnaise   Waldorf salad
Broccoli Hollandaise
Sweet trolley
Cheese
Coffee

A wonderful display for the reception, in which the flower arrangement provides a perfect backdrop for an appetizing array of food. The beautifully iced cake has a top-knot of flowers, and a garland of flowers around the base that ties in with the main arrangement. The use of a two-tier vase keeps the flowers out of the way when the food is being served.

But 150 people, she thought, were really too many to get sat down, and once they were seated they would not be able to move around and talk to anyone else. So what about a buffet? If it did turn out to be a nice day people could wander out on to the lawn with their food. The choice was now between a finger buffet with small bite-sized pieces of food ('So that's what a bouchée is!'), and a fork buffet, in which case people would need a knife and fork, and therefore little tables to sit at. She thought it was important to encourage people to mix as much as possible, and chose a finger buffet from a range of five. She liked the balanced variety, understood what it all meant, and the price was within her budget:

Fried legs of chicken
Goujon of lemon sole with Tartare sauce
Prawn bouchées
Turkey and ham vol-au-vent
Scotch eggs
Lamb cutlets
Selection of sandwiches
Asparagus tips in brown bread
Sausage rolls
Fruit salad and cream
Coffee

HIRING A HALL

You may not be like Helena – you may want to hire a hall instead, with your family or outside caterer coping with the cooking. You are still going to need to draw up a list of questions to ask, and to compare answers if there is more than one possibility:

Is the hall available when you want it, at the time you want it?

Can you have access beforehand?

How much does it cost? How much deposit must you pay? Is there any insurance cover?

Is heating included in the price? When will it be put on? Are gas, electricity and water supplied?

Are there enough cloakrooms and toilet facilities for the number of guests you have in mind?

Are chairs, tables and crockery available, or must you arrange to hire these separately?

How many parking spaces are there, and where else can people park nearby?

Who clears up afterwards? Who checks that the place is clean to start with? Is there a caretaker, and do you need to tip him?

Is there a separate kitchen? Does it have power points, a fridge, cooker, washing-up facilities, refuse disposal arrangements?

Are there any restrictions about alcohol – perhaps because it is a church hall? Do you need a licence? Does smoking invalidate insurance?

May you decorate the hall as you like?

Who is your contact, and what is his telephone number?

AT HOME

If you have a big garden – or an appropriate car park – you might want to hire a marquee. This is likely to be expensive because putting it up and taking it down are very labour-intensive, and extras, such as awnings, separate flooring and partitions, knock up the price still more. You will also have to give a thought to practical details, like time of year and temperature. If your home has only the usual 'offices', you will need a portaloo or a set of very willing neighbours.

In the *Yellow Pages*, you will find firms who hire out marquees, and other firms that supply anything from a commercial cleaner to shampoo your carpets ready for the wedding, to a cake-stand and carving knife. Whatever you need, from wine glasses and outsize flower vases, to tea urns and catering cookware, you can hire; but try borrowing first and think about alternatives. If, for example, you were to change to a finger buffet you could get rid of plates and cutlery altogether as long as you provided plentiful supplies of paper napkins. If you do resort to hiring, find out exact terms for damage or breakage, arrangements about deposits and their return; keep any receipts and copies of agreements – and make sure that those who have to take things back afterwards know where to go, that they have the paperwork, and that they realize that cardboard containers and cartons are an essential part of the product.

HIRING PEOPLE

You may want to lay on a toast-master, a coachman in full livery to drive your carriage, a commissionnaire to salute you as you come out of church, but most likely of all is a caterer. Jean and Elizabeth specialize in catering for weddings. Says Jean, 'Every wedding is different, and you never get a second chance to put things right if they go wrong.' And, adds Elizabeth, 'If only brides and their mothers would ask about the things that really matter to them, we would be able to do better still. The worst thing is that they don't always like to talk about money, and unless they do tell us what they want to spend, we can't know whether to suggest Scotch eggs and salad or salmon and strawberries.' So what should you be asking your caterer?

Are they free to do the work for your wedding when you want them?

What can they offer – a hot or cold sit-down meal, a fork or finger buffet?

How many people can they cope with?

Do they prepare food on their own premises or do they need to do on-the-spot cooking?

Do they offer a series of set dishes or do they plan the menu around your own suggestions?

How do they match what you want to the price you have set aside for catering? Can they compromise creatively? Do you pay more for diversions and digressions?

How experienced are they? Whose weddings or dinner parties have they dealt with recently?

Can they supply cutlery, crockery, a cake-stand, as well as table-cloths and glassware? Can they cope with wines?

Will they be responsible for table arrangements and flowers?

Will they serve guests and cut up the wedding cake?

What are the arrangements for deposits, payment in advance, cancellation charges, VAT, tips and insurance?

When would they like to inspect the facilities they are going to use?

DOING THINGS YOURSELF

This is the best way to cut costs as your friends and family provide their services free, and you do not have to pay VAT at 15 per cent. But it is not something for you to undertake lightly unless you have the time and the temperament. Organization has to be superb both in general and in detail: you have to rally the troops, allocate the jobs, keep written records of who is doing what, and keep on checking that everything is on schedule. In practical terms, it means that you have to be confident that Aunt Louise has the Quiche Lorraine in her freezer, that next door have at last got a new plug on their slo-cooker, that the local guides will lend you their large aluminium dixie to boil your large ham in.

Do:

prepare as much as you can in advance;

appoint a close, competent friend to be arch-organizer on the day – both you and your mother will have to opt out;

ask another friend to deal with drinks;

keep careful records and remember to hand them over;

keep accounts, and make sure you pay up promptly if you ask anyone to buy anything for you;

think about alternatives to a buffet, such as a cocktail party with canapés, or afternoon tea with scones, strawberry jam and thick cream, followed by wedding cake and a glass of Marsala for the toast;

calculate quantities carefully in your catering – your mother will not want lots of leftovers;

keep a stock of reserves in packets and tins that can be opened up quickly;

make the most of the opportunity to have your favourite food, even if it is steak and kidney pie – and do eat;

choose a co-ordinated colour scheme that fits in with existing furnishings, linking together candles, flowers, napkins;

arrange for someone to wash up and clear up afterwards, and keep mopping-up cloths, a bucket and plastic sacks handy.

Don't:

attempt it at all if you are not one hundred per cent certain that this is what you and, above all, your mother really want;

overestimate facilities or capabilities – you can have a small dinner party of six or eight controlled by the number of place settings your family table will take, perhaps thirty-five people for a buffet, up to fifty if you are hiring a hall;

be too ambitious – keep things simple;

be sensitive about accepting any offer of help or any contribution in kind;

forget to lay on transport if you are hiring a hall; and you may need hefty people to heave things around;

forget basics in the bathroom at home like paper towels, toilet rolls and soap;

forget ashtrays, unless you are actively discouraging smoking;

forget to put valuables and breakables out of sight;

leave anything to the last minute;

get too tired or harassed;

get upset by errors and omissions – turn them into a joke.

SUPPLEMENTARY SESSIONS
Even if you and your mother decide to escape from D-I-Y catering on the actual day, you will probably have a steady stream of people dropping in to bring you presents, or to wish you well. And even after a full-scale reception at a hotel, it is not unknown for the bride's mother to return home and find guests queuing at her gate. You can stock up cake tins well in advance with biscuits and shortbread to serve with tea, or with a glass of sweet white wine; or you can make sure you have supplies of titbits and nibbles to serve with chilled sherry or soft drinks.

You may also choose to entertain family and friends who are travelling some distance the evening before the wedding. Helena's family wanted to be hospitable to their daughter's future in-laws, whom they scarcely knew. So Helena's mother and aunt arranged a buffet party for thirty-five people at a cost of just over £2 a head, planned well in advance and needing the minimum of last minute attention:

French bread and home-made chicken liver pâté
Lemons stuffed with creamed smoked mackerel
Florida fruits

Sliced cold roast turkey
Sliced cold honeyroast ham
Salami platter
Tuna fish quiche
Quiche Lorraine
Green salad, beansprouts and peaches salad, mushroom salad,
red bean salad with peppers, tomato and onion salad

Lemon soufflé
Frosted ginger cake
Crème brulée
Cream of apricot Chantilly

WHICH WINE WILL IT BE?

Wine increases the price of a reception more than anything, but you can control quality and consumption by consultation and careful planning. Spirits, the most expensive and heavily-taxed drinks of all, are 'out' at wedding receptions, though you might want to have them at a pay-bar for a dance or disco during the evening. You will probably see your wine 'programme' for the reception in three stages.

First, something to keep people happy, to hand to them when they first arrive. A glass of sherry, dry or medium, offered on a silver tray; the driest is Fino, which is delicious chilled in summer, and the medium is usually labelled Amontillado but sometimes Oloroso in Britain. You will get about twelve glasses out of the usual 75 cl bottle. You will also need beer and lager, maybe cider, and chilled fruit juices and soft drinks for children and non-drinkers.

Second, an accompaniment to the meal. The rigid rules of white with fish and red with most meats have gone for good, so you can operate on a basis of real personal preference. Usually you find, though, that at parties two out of three people opt for white. If you are like Helena and do not know much about choosing wines, consult the experts, but keep control of your costs. If you are on your own, you can consider as good buys and generally acceptable wines:

Whites: Californian, Hungarian, Yugoslav Riesling
Reds: Californian, Italian Valpolicella

Some of these come in large bottles – much larger than the usual 70 or 75 cl – and these are a better buy than wine boxes, where you pay a lot for the package, do not necessarily get a good wine, and encourage over-consumption through self-help as people just love playing with little taps. You should allow about half a 75 cl bottle for each guest.

Third, wine for the toast that will go with the cake: perhaps a sparkling white wine from Italy, like Asti Spumante served well-chilled; or Moscato which comes from the same region but is cheaper because it does not have an Asti label; or Veuve du Vernay from France. You should get six glasses out of each bottle.

There are infinite variations on the wine theme, with interludes for juices, soft drinks, Perrier water, beer and lager. You may of course want to celebrate with champagne throughout, when you will need to allow half to three-quarters of a bottle for each person, with about six glasses in each bottle. If the word 'Brut' appears on the label, it is a very dry champagne. This would not be a good choice to go with wedding cake, which needs something sweeter, indicated by the words 'demi-sec'. You will also find these words used to describe the much cheaper sparkling wines – such as Blanquette de Limoux – which are also made by the champagne method. It is up to you, bearing in mind the lament of an experienced organizer: 'It was such a lovely wedding. It's a pity none of them remembered it.'

'BAKE ME A CAKE...AS FAST AS YOU CAN'

Kathy's cake turned out to be cardboard. Actually, after the initial shock she did not mind at all, because she and Sam had beautiful photographs of themselves posing by a seven-tier model. The problem was that the confectioner had slipped up, in spite of Kathy's repeated checks, and had not top-iced the cake in time. Apologetically, the manager offered to lend her their best demonstration model, a real architectural creation of cardboard and foam plastic. And no one was aware of what had happened, as Kathy's own basic white cake was cut up by the caterer after the toast. And as far as Kathy was concerned, she knew she was much better off than her friend Bess, who had seen her pillars tilt and slowly sink down through soft icing.

A CHECK-LIST FOR THE CAKE

How many people do you need to serve at the reception; and how many neighbours and friends do you want to give or send cake to afterwards? Confectioners who cut up cake have a 'standard' to go by, whereas non-professionals, like the ladies who cut up Helena's cake, were over-generous and there was no cake left to send away (perhaps because one young man proudly boasted he had had five pieces). You should also consider the high cost of postage when sending cake away.

What sort of cake? Is it to be a classic rich fruit cake, or do you want something different, like a biscuit wheat sheaf, a white frosted Swiss roll stuffed with glacé cherries, or a French pyramid of profiteroles?

What style and shape? Is it to be square, round, heart-shaped? Go cake-shopping to collect ideas: look at displays in bakers' windows; demonstrations given by catering colleges; consult bride magazines and cookery books.

How many tiers do you want? Are you going to be traditionally British and use pillars (round pillars for a round cake and square ones for a square cake), or are you going to adopt the American idea of having the tiers sit directly on top of each other, with the cake usually made of a lighter Madeira mixture? Are you intending to put a tier away for an anniversary or christening? A rich fruit cake will keep long enough in an airtight tin, but white icing yellows with age. Royal custom is to strip off old icing and re-ice for a christening.

Do you need to ask the confectioner to make an extra square or round to be produced, ready cut-up for the reception?

This traditional, three-tiered cake forms a spectacular centre-piece at the reception.

A cake with a difference. If you are having an untraditional type of wedding reception, you can choose any style and shape of wedding cake, such as this one in the shape of two interlocking hearts.

Who will bake and make your cake? Will it be:
- home-made and home-iced;
- home-made and professionally iced;
- made entirely by a bakery chain;
- made entirely by a specialist celebration-cake artist?

A home-made cake is the cheapest and most likely the best-quality cake, but you should not assume that a specialist's charges are necessarily higher than those of a bakery chain. Ask around – and ask to taste a sample. Your criteria for choosing are likely to be based on skills available (your own?), price, and the value you put on appearance – perhaps at the expense of taste.

How do you match up what you really want with what you can afford, and with what is available at the exact time you want it?

Whatever you choose, it will be the centre-piece of your celebration, even if it has less than seven tiers. And it is not only a visibly decorative centre-piece, as original and as personal as you want to make it, but it is also a symbol. It is part of an age-old tradition in which a cake – or even once upon a time a wheaten biscuit – represented fertility and plenty in marriage.

AND THE BRIDE WORE ... 'SILK, SATIN, MUSLIN, RAGS'

The first decision you need to make when choosing your wedding dress is, to what extent will you be governed by tradition? What is the truth about tradition? Brides were not expected to wear white until the sixteenth century, and even then – because of the high cost of clothes – girls tended to resort to their best dress, whatever its colour. Moreover, though Roman women wore saffron yellow veils at their weddings, the veil as we know it today did not appear until the middle of the nineteenth century. So you are free to define tradition as you like, or to concentrate on current fashion, accepting and flouting, with your choice wide open from jeans and jersey to a Scarlett O'Hara hooped skirt, floppy hat and parasol. New, finer fabrics of man-made fibres, a variety of mixtures, new processes, new technology, give you a range of choice that would never have been possible a generation ago, with speed of production – copies of the royal wedding dress were available the day after the wedding – and a wide range of prices. Brides have never been so free in their choice, and they may sometimes feel that there is too much of it.

MIXING AND MATCHING

Whatever you choose, you are likely to have some general theme or scheme in mind which will visually bind together your family and friends, with your dress as the focus of attention. Perhaps you have set your heart on a real country wedding, a military or naval wedding, or one based on your tennis or cricket club or on some other shared interest. Alternatively, you may pick on particular colours to highlight. Sandra combined the two: she wanted an Edwardian theme with creams and reds and the shiny green of aspidistras as her dominant colour scheme. So she and her three bridesmaids wore long cream dresses and straw boaters trimmed and tied with tulle and garlands of small red and orange flowers; the two mothers collaborated, one wearing a deeper cream suit and the other a light tan dress and jacket – but both drew the line at wearing boaters. The colours and style were followed through in bouquets, flower arrangements in church and on the tables for the buffet lunch, and with orange and red rugs on the lawn and wine in wicker hampers.

Integration is the keyword; and it applies most of all to the details of your own complete outfit. You will not look or feel good if you follow a pot luck, piecemeal kind of approach. Hat or head-dress, your hair, and your veil are interdependent: all parts of one unit. You can horrify yourself by imagining that you are seriously considering four dresses, that you like two head-dresses, and you quite fancy three veils, though you still wonder whether you would not be happier with just a circlet of flowers. There are thirty-two different combinations possible: four (dresses) × four (veils; one being the choice of no veil at all) × two (head-dresses) = thirty-two. You will have to form your own guide-lines by trial and error to reach even this stage, resisting all pressure from other people. You will have some idea of what suits you in a dress, and you will be keenly aware of the reality of your own figure, of what needs hiding and what needs highlighting. However, you are not used to parading around in veils and head-dresses, and it can come as quite a shock to see yourself in them for the first time. You have to do the same type of self-appraisal as with a dress, counterbalancing a long thin face, for example, by small bunches of flowers in your hair at cheek-bone level.

WHAT TO WATCH OUT FOR WHEN BUYING

You are going to spend a considerable amount of money; the average is around £150, though you could go to an Oxfam shop and get a nearly-new dress for £10, or you could pay £1000 for a special creation of the finest silk. Whatever the price, your wedding dress is likely to be the most expensive dress you have ever bought – a dress promoted and packaged to sell dreams, but still a commercially-produced garment designed, cut out, machined and finished like other products of the rag trade. It is hard for other people to put a price on a dress: a survey of 'little black dresses' proved that it is very difficult to tell the difference between a cheap chain-store dress at one extreme and a designer dress at the other. So you have the consolation, if you need it, that no one will know with any certainty how much you have paid. You pay for originality, individuality, quality of fabric and finish, but a mass-produced model worn by you in your own special way with your variation of accessories will not be instantly recognizable.

Do:

look around at what is available within the price range you have set for your own dress and its accessories and those of your bridesmaids. Consult magazines, look at dress patterns, gaze in shop windows, appraising critically rather than concentrating solely on filmy floatings down the aisle; try on friends' dresses – even your mother's. Above all, get ideas – practical, possible ideas;

try on a variety of styles, shades, colours, lengths, assessing and comparing, getting a general impression of what you can expect for the money you have in mind;

take a second opinion along – someone who shares the same tastes as you, and who does not easily get bored or irritable. Tactful explanations may be in order to mothers who are denied their 'rightful' expectations;

make a list of points the shop, salon or 'house' needs to know to carry out their job properly: the date and time of your wedding (artificial light affects colours); the date by which you need your dress (perhaps for an 'official' studio portrait the day before); how much you intend to spend and how the money is to be allocated for accessories and bridesmaids' or page boys' outfits;

wear the bra and belt you intend to set aside for the day; and if it is a strapless bra, check up that the bodice does not somehow drag it agonizingly downwards. Take along your slip and find out whether it is antistatic – you do not want your dress clinging compulsively to your knees. If it is a winter wedding, think about your 'thermals' and make sure the size of your gown takes into account any extra layers. There is nothing worse than being cold;

wear shoes with the height and type of heel you find most appropriately comfortable, and get the length of your skirt perfect – it's very easy to tread on or trip over just a very few centimetres of extra length;

check up on detail, even if on this occasion you are not looking for durability: is the zip well sewn in and does it run freely without the material catching? Is the stitching straight, particularly if pin tucks are a feature of the bodice, and the seams unpuckered? Are buttons sewn on firmly and the buttonholes tidy? Are the belt-loops wide enough to avoid crushing the fabric, and is the level perfect?

value your comfort – you have got to be able to walk, breathe, kneel down and eat. Check that any supporting structure – any boning or wiring – does not dig in and that seams, particularly under your arms, do not scratch. Arline walked out of one shop where the assistant remarked, 'Well, you won't be wearing it for long, dear', when she pointed out a rough seam that had chafed her skin after only a few seconds;

try on the dress and all its accessories; do not be embarrassed about taking along a veil, a head-dress, and white lacy gloves (to hide those 'housework' hands!) that you have borrowed or even bought somewhere else;

consider the special importance of your backview since people will be looking at it for a long time. Does the dress flow and fall well from your waist? Is there some interesting detail to focus on? Are the veil and train in harmony with the whole?

ask about fitting arrangements – how many will you need and when will they be? Can you plan them to fit in with your schedule? And what about alterations, their price and their timing ('time is of the essence')? How are special problems dealt with, like a last minute loss of weight?

check on cancellation policies and methods of payment. A credit card gives you more time to pay, and certain bank cards give extra legal protection;

remember that even the most reputable and exclusive bridal houses have sales from time to time;

when you finally get your dress home – collected or delivered – go over it from top to toe; do not be satisfied with second best.

How do you choose between all the different dresses that are available? Do try on as many different styles, shades and lengths of dress as you can, to get a general impression of what you want. And from the start consider what head-dress, shoes and accessories you want to wear.

Don't

be rushed – start looking around three or even five months before you are to be married, and do not go shopping when you are tired or harassed;

be bulldozed, bamboozled, misguided, misled, just to enable someone to make a quick sale;

go shopping at peak times, if you can help it;

be vague about what is included in the price; do not be afraid to talk about money. If you need a slightly longer dress, for example, will there be an extra charge?

buy unless you get a firm guarantee about delivery dates and alteration times in writing;

deprive your bridesmaids of time to make their choice and the opportunity to have their say, especially if they are paying;

choose a fabric that crushes easily – it is vital that any creases drop out instantly;

hang up your dress when you get it home, especially if it is made of stretch fabric – you do not want an uneven, unintentionally frilly edge. Lay it out flat, perhaps on the spare bed, and press it the day before your wedding taking care to use the right temperature in order not to get a molten mass of nylon organza on the bottom of your iron;

forget to scrutinize your dress and accessories for any damage, defects and imperfections. Look for grease marks on the neckline and cuffs, smears of someone else's lipstick, and pulled threads. Take a close look at embroidery, appliqué, and the threading and fastening off of any bead work;

forget that, though this is your dream of a dress, it is still something that is being bought and sold, and which you choose for objective as well as subjective reasons. Do not buy until you are certain; if in doubt, leave it out.

SUITING YOURSELF

You have to take yourself as you are; indeed, it is important to like yourself as you are, plus or minus a few pounds. You presumably will not be making drastic alterations to your hair colour or skin tone, so look for a dress that really fits in with the girl your fiancé fell in love with. Do not just assume you will have a *white* wedding. After all, what is white? One dressmaker alleges that there are over one hundred different shades. Dead white drains away colour from a pale skin; in fact it is difficult for anyone to wear except perhaps the truly bronzed sun-worshippers, and their tans can fade fast and unevenly before the wedding day. Cream is not necessarily kind either; it makes sallowish skins look rather muddy. So you do have to try out a whole range of whites, ivories and creams, and the different textures of fabrics will affect the shades as well. If you are beginning to despair, try a short or three-quarter length dress, as there is less white to overwhelm you. Or consider a hint of colour: pale apricot piping, for example; or stiffly starched broderie anglaise threaded through with pale blue ribbon; or a rose-coloured taffeta petticoat with ruffles or flounces underneath silk organza, chiffon or voile; or even – flouting those traditions of doubtful historical origin – have a dress in your favourite pastel colour with your flowers of a deeper shade to tone in.

And what about your shape and size? Know yourself, be honest: do not ask for a size 12 when you know very well that you can only just squeeze into a 14; above all, accept expert help in turning a defect into an asset. If you are roundish, short and bouncy, you should avoid frills and flounces, puffed sleeves and any trimmings that seem to split you in two; instead, emphasize your elegantly curving shoulders, choose a plain high neckline or a mandarin collar, and a waistline that tapers off to a 'V'. If your hips are wide, try out a loosely cut dress (it does not have to look like maternity wear or your grandmother's nightie), which does not cling to and clutter up your waistline: perhaps a Jane Austen style in a soft fabric flowing from a high bust-line, with smooth straight central panels. If you are tall and thin, you can experiment with trimmings round your dress – scallops round a crinoline, or a layered look. The general principle is to create a diversion, a counter-attraction, and always to bear in mind that the model girls who show off wedding gowns in magazines or at mannequin parades are chosen for their proportions, perfection and photogenic reaction. They are not you. Nor do you wish to be them.

SEVEN BRIDES FOR . . . SEVEN DRESSES

Betsy had been to dressmaking classes and was now quite competent in cutting out and sewing summer clothes. But a wedding dress was quite a different matter. She knew she could get a cut-out, ready-to-sew dress, even one specially designed for her, but that was not quite enough of a challenge. So she found a paper pattern that she liked – a plain princess line with a long, zipped back – and stuck to professional instructions about trying it out first in cheap muslin before facing up to the shimmering ivory satin that she had in mind. However, her practice run turned out so well, and the dress fitted her so perfectly, that she had not the heart to throw it out and start all over again. So she got married in her muslin, stiffening it with spray-on starch, sewing on pearly plastic sequins, and running up a rustling pale pink underskirt.

Nora knew she would never get around to dyeing her dress afterwards, and that it would just continue to clutter up her cupboard; she could not be bothered with black bags and large sheets of tissue paper. For her, the solution was hiring not just the dress but the whole outfit at one go, so that she could be sure everything matched. She did not have much time either, and was glad to find that the photographer she had booked also hired out dresses. He boasted that he had more than four hundred to choose from. The first rack Nora looked at displayed dresses that were decidedly tatty, mildly yellowing in places, and clearly needed to be pensioned off; but the others were indistinguishable from new in their plastic bags, each one with suggestions for matching accessories. She was in and out and happy, back at work before the morning was over, with firm arrangements made to collect her dress two days before the wedding. And she knew that the photographer really had the knack of arranging that train which she had not expected to like, until she tried it on.

Corinne had watched the 'Crossroads' television wedding and knew that the bride had got married in a real off-the-peg, chain store wedding dress. So, as a starting point, she went off to the nearest branch and found a good range of styles in all the standard sizes for both-brides and bridesmaids: and that was that. The

A traditional wedding calls for a traditional wedding gown. This classic outfit consists of a dress trimmed around the waist and hem, with a built-in train, worn with a long veil falling from a close-fitting head-dress.

There are many alternatives to the traditional wedding dress. The important point is to choose something that suits your own style.

fifth dress she tried on she knew was hers exactly as it was, made from yards of softly floating, sprigged organdie with billowing bouffant sleeves, and the high, gently frilled collar she knew she needed because her neck always went red and blotchy when she was nervous. She looked at herself in the long mirror: 'Just like patient Griselda,' she murmured,

> 'She stood transmuted by her wondrous dress
> Almost unrecognized through loveliness.'

Is it really me?

Davina decided she would try out the nearest branch of a shop specializing in bridal wear. She liked the idea that it was not a national chain; she had even seen its shops in Paris, so she reckoned it must be good and really in touch with fashion to keep up with the taste and flair of those chic French women. She wanted an overview of the coming spring fashions and the chance to find out how the latest trends fitted in with her own particular fancies; she also wanted the opportunity to mix and match and fit together her accessories, and the security of sound advice to give her self-confidence. She thought someone in the shop must have a sense of humour as there was a neatly printed notice: 'No prams, please'. Which dress would it be? They all had names: Lucinda and Lolita, Cathérine or Clothilde, Geraldine or Geneviève. She liked these names: they made choosing more real, more personal and certainly a good deal easier when she came to use the pairing system. Yes, it was Geneviève, and though it was really nothing to do with her reason for choosing it, she did like that French name which made her think of King Arthur, and she loved the silky sheen of her dress falling in layered folds, its baby puff sleeves, and the filled-in lace bodice which tightly fitted her tiny waist. This was it – at a price. 'I never should have let myself look at this range', she told herself. 'But now it's just too late.'

Bridget sent off for a series of brochures from individual 'houses' or salons, and she picked out the one whose styles she liked best, and which happened to involve the least travelling. She looked at and tried on specimen dresses at many different prices, and picked out features from several that she liked so that these could all be combined into her own, very special dress – at no extra cost. She liked the way in which her visit to the salon was by appointment to suit her and her mother (who reclined elegantly on an eighteenth-century sofa), and the fact that only one family at a time was dealt with. She had to have two fittings; even though these were on Saturday afternoons, both the fitter and the seamstress were there to help and advise.

Debbie's dress of pure Thai silk turned out to be one of the cheapest of the seven gowns. She saw a design that she liked in a British bride magazine, worked out her own modifications, took careful measurements; and then, far away in a small open-fronted shop in a back street of Bangkok, a diminutive dressmaker sat cross-legged on the floor and worked away at the rich ivory silk, setting tiny tucks down the bodice, piping a high collar, carefully planning the inset train, which started with fine pleats at the waist, fanning out into wider pleats flowing out into a semi-circle. The two bridesmaids had similar dresses in crimson silk, without trains but with finely pleated bows to give interest to the back. And now Debbie's photograph has pride of place in that little shop in Surwonge Road.

Tina had very little money, but she still wanted a long white dress, so she scoured the second-hand columns of the small ads in the local newspaper. Here was one with a difference:

'Wedding dress and all accessories, size 12, calf length, full skirt, white broderie anglaise, never worn, £50, Little Hinscomb 3785 after 6.'

Never worn; why ever not? thought Tina. Had the girl been jilted, had she changed her mind at the last minute? So Tina telephoned for an appointment. A middle-aged woman greeted her. 'I've come about the dress', said Tina. It fitted her like a dream and her eyes moistened at the sight of herself. The woman looked at her longingly, turned and ran sobbing out of the bedroom. The dress, she explained, had been her daughter's, and she had died of leukaemia two weeks before her wedding. 'You look so like her', whispered the mother, 'take the dress as my gift to you. Wear it for her. Make it a happy dress.' Tina took the dress – and it was a happy dress worn for herself and also worn in memory of a girl she had never known, a girl who had looked like her.

'SLOW-DROPPING VEILS OF THINNEST LAWN'

A veil is the item that you are most likely to borrow, perhaps from your mother or even from your grandmother: and that is when you begin to inherit the problems of antiquity, of delicate fragility needing skilled repairs, of discolouration needing expert laundry, the points of intricate lace being pinned out to dry flat on a board like a frog laid out on a dissecting table. You may find that an old veil, far from being made of Tennyson's 'thinnest lawn', consists of quite solid Bruxelles, Bruges or Honiton lace that might look better incorporated into a dress than used as a head covering. The revolution in veils came after World War II, when the finest nylon threads began to be spun into a diversity of light, cobwebby, floating fabrics, creating new styles and new trends at low prices. There is much more incentive to add the mystery of arriving at the church with a veil over your face if your veil adds a soft touch of romantic mistiness, rather than the thick shrouding of an old-fashioned net curtain. Tradition is not, however, strongly in favour of veiled brides because there was, historically, the fear of some unfortunate bridegroom being married off to a substitute bride!

If you do decide to wear a veil, there is a great variety to choose from: full frothy veils, perhaps with several layers; short, waist length, or full length veils; veils incorporated into a train or flowing from a juliet cap; veils embroidered and embossed, jimped and scalloped; all in shades to match your dress. Princess Diana wore a long, silk net veil embroidered with 10,000 mother-of-pearl sequins, toning in with her creamy silk Emmanuel gown. Remember that the longer the veil, the more problems you will have with weight, drag, and the worry of someone behind you standing on it. You will have to practise walking to get used to it. Moreover, you do have to bear in mind that your veil and head-dress (whether coronet, tiara, clasp of pearls, silken band or garland of flowers) are one unit and have to take the strain if you decide to start off with your face veiled, and then dramatically throw back your veil in the vestry. Make sure your chief bridesmaid has time to produce a comb and pocket mirror.

Your hair, too, is an integral part of veil and head-dress, and you will obviously want an early consultation with your regular hairdresser, who understands the way you are. It may even happen that your hair becomes the dominant feature: you may want to plait in ropes of pearls, or to weave in flowers fixed to matching – or white – hair grips or side combs. You can try out small sprays of silk flowers, or fresh ones like freesias, periwinkles, lilies of the valley, or florets from hyacinths, or any flowers that have stout calyxes or stalks so that they can be wired.

Instead of having a veil and head-dress, you may want to make a dominant feature of your hair. If you have long hair, you can plait in ropes of pearls or ribbons, or weave flowers into it.

FEET FIRST . . . BOOTS, SHOES, SLIPPERS, CLOGS

Walk down any High Street, or London's Oxford Street, and you will be surrounded by shoe shops. Why do you choose one and not another? Popular reasons include a liking for particular styles stocked, value for money, range of sizes and widths – and expert fitting. For your wedding day, it will be style and colour or shade that catch your eye first, but in the last resort comfort is most important: you are going to spend hours on your feet, and a little nip here or a small pinch there, a bit of slop at the heel minutely perceived in the shop, will not improve with time, and you will end up with blisters. The sincerity and serenity of your smile are going to crack if your feet hurt, though you can always take the precaution of getting your bridesmaid to bring along a pair of tried and tested shoes for you to slip into after the vanity of public parade and photographs has been appeased. However, if you do not like the idea of your bridesmaid tripping

One of the most important of all the decisions that you have to make about your wedding day is what to wear on your feet. You will probably want to wear a pretty pair of shoes that go well with your dress, but do make sure that they will be comfortable to walk and stand in for several hours.

down the aisle with a shoe bag on her arm, go to a shop featuring fitting skills, particularly if your feet deviate in the slightest from the so-called standard.

In the interests of comfort you may decide not to buy new shoes at all, but to wear a pair of old, familiar ones. If you do want new shoes, however, you will find that the reasons for your final choice are a mixed bag of personal whims and fancies, the constraints and limitations of the general situation, and sound common sense: you will, for example, see style in relation to your dress – do you need court shoes, ankle straps, open sandals, ballet-style slippers, white kid or suède short boots for a three-quarter length winter gown? You will see height of heel, and the broadness of its base, not only in relation to your dress but in relation to your bridegroom: remember the 'flatties' that Princess Diana so elegantly wore? Colour, too, is not a matter of free choice, for it depends on the shade of white you choose for your dress or the contrast you opt for to link up with trimmings, flowers or even bridesmaids' dresses. You could be daring and choose crimson shoes to match the red of your roses and the bridesmaids' colour scheme. And if the exact colour you want is difficult to obtain (pastel shades and unusual colours can be hard to get) try dyeing a cheap pair of chain-store shoes; you can also glue on glitter, stitch on velvet and diamanté bows, sew on sequins, stencil your intertwining initials or little hearts – the scope for your creativity is enormous. Your choice, too, will depend on what you intend to use them for afterwards: do you see them for ever laid to rest in their wrappings, do you see them as future evening wear, as best shoes, or as practical general-purpose shoes?

Do remember:

Try on your shoes – old or new – with your dress when you are choosing it;

Consider the harmony of the whole picture you are creating;

Practise walking about;

Wear your shoes in advance to break them in;

Make sure the soles are not slippery – scratch the surface with an old poker, add feather-light stick-on sole tips and heels, or even paint the soles with clear polyurethane;

Check that any fastenings, like little buttons on elastic or buckles, are well sewn on. Put your dress on before your shoes, and even then watch out for the sharp prongs of buckles;

Take a look in the sales if you have a long lead-in period, particularly if you want white shoes at the end of the summer;

Remove the price ticket: do not kneel down at the altar with 'reduced to £10.99' glaring at the congregation.

'SAY IT WITH FLOWERS'

Claire could not get fresh flowers for her wedding. She had made countless calls and visits to nurseries, florists, specialist flower-arrangers, but always the answer was 'no'. Her problem? She was getting married on Easter Monday and in her part of the North-West the flower markets and the retail outlets they supplied were all closed from Good Friday until Easter Tuesday. What was she going to do? She did not want imitation flowers. Despairing and downcast, she trudged home chilled by the bleak February wind, past the long queues of patient visitors outside the district hospital waiting for opening time, each one clutching a bunch of flowers. Flowers . . . florists. Which florist? She peered at the name on a piece of discarded wrapping paper – a little shop just round the corner. 'Oh, we never close. As long as the hospital is open, we're open. Yes, even on Bank Holidays.' And so it came about that the young woman at the florists worked all day on Easter Sunday making up bouquets and sprays from the long-lasting, tight-budded blooms she had bought at Thursday's market. So Claire had her flowers, but her advice is: do not get married on a Bank Holiday.

'AND HER ARMS FULL OF FLOWERS'

Where do you begin? Claire's starting point was her bouquet. When she had settled on that – a posy of lilies of the valley, small yellow Singapore orchids, yellow and white carnations sprigged with rosemary and edged with leaves of variegated ivy – everything else fell harmoniously into place: her bridesmaids carried sweet-smelling pomanders spiked with yellow jasmine and miniature daffodils; the two mothers wore sprays of yellow and white orchids, and Claire's father, the bridegroom and his best man wore white carnations; the decorations for the church, to supplement the magnificent arum lilies that already graced the altar, were worked out with the regular team of church 'flower ladies' and included branches of white cherry blossom and forsythia, white lilac and mimosa from the South of France, and a host of daffodils picked from the garden and from the field by the little stream where Claire used to play; and finally, for her reception, she had small posies of primroses and wild daffodils on the tables and a central tiered arrangement, all following her spring-time theme, with garlands of green ivy from the old oak tree in the family garden looped round the sparkling white linen table-cloths and knotted with yellow and white nylon net bows inset with jasmine. On top of her cake she put the small fluted silver vase that her mother had used at her wedding, filled with dog violets, freesia buds and lilies of the valley.

WHAT'S THE POINT OF FLOWERS?

Claire could think of a number of reasons why she wanted flowers, and they were so important that she reached the stage when she did not inquire about price. 'Well, it's tradition, isn't it? Girls have always carried flowers of some sort, perhaps because flowers stand for something – like red roses meaning "I love you"; white flowers are supposed to symbolize innocence, and purple ones, which I quite fancied if only I had been able to get hold of some of those sprays of rich purple Thai orchids, the blood of Christ. Anyway, flowers are beautiful in

A striking effect is achieved when colours and styles are well co-ordinated. You should wait until you have chosen your own and your bridesmaids' dresses before thinking about bouquets. You need to match the colours of the flowers to those in the dresses; in addition, you should match the size and style of the bouquets to the styles of the dresses, to achieve a balanced and integrated effect.

themselves, and carrying a bouquet will make me feel more beautiful – and what else would I do with my hands? I might pick or even bite my nails and fidget with my fingers. And from the guests' point of view, flowers give them something to focus on while they are waiting. Flowers create the right sort of feeling, the same as music does. It's also quite a big church, so I shall use bird cherry to cordon off the two central aisles where the congregation will sit. And there's a monstrous brass lectern with an enormous eagle which used to frighten the life out of me when I was little – I can't move him but I can discreetly hide him. On the other hand, there's a stained-glass window that always fascinated me – I'd like to feature that with a very special flower arrangement. All this is part of me as I was, as I am.'

How you rate flowers is obviously very personal, your choice depending on the value you put on flowers and the amount you are prepared to spend. Expenditure can range from almost nothing (if you limit yourself to a single red rose carried with conviction), to over £150 for bouquets, corsages and full-scale

arrangements in church and at your reception. You can cut costs by choosing flowers that are actually in season in this country, by planning to share the cost of decorating the church with other brides who are getting married on the same day, by picking a time of year – like harvest festival – when the church will be decorated anyway, by using wild flowers and woodland greenery as Claire did, and by growing flowers yourself and raiding other people's gardens – even if you do balk at actually making your own bouquet. Marguerite's mother, though, working on a very tight budget, made a beautifully simple posy: mindful of the meaning of her daughter's name she used pink, white and deep red pyrethrums, Shasta daisies and tiny bellis daisies for the centre. She found she could hide her mistakes with a doyley for edging, kitchen foil to cover the stalks, and strategically-placed twists and trails of florists' ribbon to tone in. She probably broke all the rules in the book, but it was a bouquet made with love. And there was never another like it.

Above left *A circlet of fresh flowers is an unusual and attractive alternative to a veil or head-dress.*

Above right *You may feel that a small bouquet would go better with your dress, and be easier to manage, than a large one. Have a look at the wide range of styles and sizes available before you make a decision.*

WHAT DO YOU WANT?

Do you want flowers at all? If you do, which of Claire's categories – bouquets, sprays, buttonholes, church and reception displays – are you going to choose and how do you rank your priorities? If you decide against flowers – after all, you may be allergic to pollen – you may want to consider alternatives: a white leather prayer-book or Bible, a parasol, a pomander, a dorothy bag with a draw string; or, like one Easter bride, a woven basket filled with painted Easter eggs and cotton wool chickens. Perhaps, like Claire, you feel you need something to do with your hands!

Do you want a bouquet of real or imitation flowers, and is it to be an off-the-peg standard bouquet, in which case you see exactly what you will get, or one made to your own specification. A decision on real or artificial flowers for head-dresses is often more practical than personal, depending on the time of day of your wedding, and the need to deal with the attachment of head-dress to veil and their arrangement. In any case, you can get hand-made imitation flowers in a variety of fabrics to match those of your bouquet, or you can opt for a circlet of pearls or rhinestones, or a diamanté tiara.

What style of bouquet? Here you are in unfamiliar territory again; but you can get some ideas from books or even classes on flower-arranging, from bride and women's magazines, from flower shows and from shop windows where you can study examples of artistry. There are fashions in flowers; modern bouquets tend to be smaller, softer, less formal, less massively structured arrangements, than those in the past. At the same time, your bouquet has to fit in with you, to be part of your personality, and it has to feel right physically – try holding several of different shapes and sizes, and do not let your arms droop limply down below your waistline. Your bouquet must also suit the overall impression you are creating, appropriate to a formal, classic, society wedding; a real country event; a simple, jolly, friendly family affair; or something historical – Victorian, Empire or Edwardian. And you will want to take into account your general colour scheme, your favourite flowers, your sentimentality, and the particular time of year: autumn, for example, might move you towards yellows, oranges and bronzes in rich warming colours, which you probably would not choose if you wanted a contrast with the heat of high summer.

The choice, of course, remains yours, but who is going to take overall responsibility for carrying it out? You can hire a professional at a price to organize all the flowers, or you can opt for a multiple approach using a local florist to supply sprays and bouquets, decorating the church yourself with the 'resident' flower-arrangers, and getting the hotel or restaurant to deal with the reception. There are plenty of opportunities for D-I-Y experiments according to the skills available among family and friends, who will have particular scope if your reception is in a hall or at home. Remember that you can hire not only large pots and vases, but also plants and shrubs, from some florists and also from commercial contractors, who are used to dealing with conferences and banquets.

As soon as you decide to use a commercial – and professional – service, there are questions for you to work out, such as:

Are the flowers you want going to be available? If there is any doubt, discuss acceptable substitutes at the start;

Can the florist cope with your order, however large or small, on the day you get married?

Can they advise you about styles of bouquets if you are uncommitted? What sort of 'standard' range do they have? And if you want something non-standard, can they design it?

If you have special needs, like a fresh flower head-dress, can they deal with them? If it is at all possible, do take along a sample of your wedding dress material so that colours can be matched in;

Does the price fit in with your budget? If not, where can you make economies? Ask for an itemized, not an overall, price;

Is the firm a member of a professional organization?

Will they deliver on the day, or must you arrange to collect your flowers?

Are they quite clear, in the case of promised delivery, about your address? Try to avoid using more than one address throughout the transaction.

'WITH RINGS ON HER FINGERS . . .'

Maybe the million-dollar diamond that Richard Burton gave to Liz Taylor was the exception, but wedding jewelry is not normally a good financial investment, and diamonds are far from being a girl's best friend. *Which?* magazine bought a selection of diamonds, and did not get any more for them in 1980 than they had paid ten years earlier. It would have been better to put the money in a building society since none of the stones came anywhere near giving the return needed to keep up with inflation. Still, investment, at least in money terms, is not your main aim in acquiring either an engagement or a wedding ring.

Once again, you are caught up in symbolism, significance and slowly evolving rituals and traditions. These can matter much more than money. The earliest examples of wedding rings are Roman, and were made of iron, representing the durability of marriage; they were also a sign that a down payment and a contract had been made. The tradition passed on to Britain, where rings began to be fashioned in a variety of metals and materials, including leather, reeds and rushes, the completeness of the circle showing love flowing in a continuous stream. Two matching rings, one for the bride and one for the groom, suggest togetherness, and our present tradition follows on the sixteenth-century idea of a gimmal – a double ring with two hoops seemingly inseparably joined together by a kind of clasp – which was split at the time of betrothal and the halves later united as the bride's wedding ring. Exactness of fit means harmony and perfection; never taking the ring off determines permanence; and the placing of the ring on the third finger of the left hand recalls the ancient Egyptian belief that the *vena amoris* – the vein of love – ran directly from the heart to the tip of the third finger. Today the wedding ring is at the heart of the Church marriage service; it is blessed by the clergyman and the bridegroom puts it on the bride's finger as a token of the promises they make. The bridegroom, too, can choose to wear a ring and this will also be blessed as part of the ceremony.

Here again you are faced with a commercial transaction (on which there is a high retail mark up and hefty Value Added Tax) that you have not made before. You are in the hands of specialists for whom selling jewelry, creating and caring for it, is a life work. You will probably feel ignorant and inferior; several brides admit that ring-choosing expeditions were not the pleasure they ought to have been, and one bridegroom felt sick during the process. However, you can build up your background knowledge – and therefore your self-confidence – and master the jargon in advance.

First of all, what is a carat? It is the unit of measurement of gold refinement – and indeed of other precious metals – and is an indication of the fineness of gem stones. Pure gold (not to be confused with 'real' gold) is 24 carat. However, this is much too soft for a ring that has to take the hard knocks of daily life, so it is mixed with another metal – such as brass, copper or silver – which controls the final colour of the 'mixture' or alloy. So down the scale you go to 18 carat, much advertised for wedding rings because the proportions of metals are ideal for the more creative designs that skilled craftsmen excel at. Eighteen carat is still expensive, so you may want to move on to 9 carat, which is the most hard-wearing of all. There is an excellent range for you to reflect upon in every high street jewellers. You might take a peek at platinum, which is the most costly precious metal of all, or, if you want white gold – perhaps to team up with an engagement ring – you will need gold mixed with an alloy of nickel.

Secondly, what is a hallmark? This is a guarantee that you are not being cheated. It has always been possible to debase precious metals relatively easily. Gold wedding rings must – under the Hallmarking Act of 1973 – be sold hallmarked, although slender, delicate engagement rings may be exempt. You will find a row of tiny letters and pictures stamped on articles made of gold, silver and platinum (the voluntary tradition of stamping gold and silver going back to 1238). The hallmark is made up of five small symbols; and if you look carefully you will see: the manufacturer's initials; a crown; a number telling you the carat (like 6/24, i.e., 18 carat); an assay office mark identifying the place where the ring was tested (a leopard for the London office, an anchor for Birmingham, a rose for Sheffield, a castle for Edinburgh); and, finally, an alphabetically coded date stamp, with K representing 1984. If you do not see a hallmark, do not buy that ring. Traders selling articles made of precious metals must display a notice describing hallmarks; if they fail to do so, they are breaking the law.

'AND WHAT SHALL WE DO FOR A RING?'

One thing is certain: you will not, unlike the Owl and the Pussycat, find a convenient piggywig 'with a ring through the end of his nose'. You will have to go out and buy a ring, whether from the local jeweller who sold you your first

Snoopy watch, from a national chain, a specialist shop, or even by mail order. There is nothing in the law which compels you to have a wedding ring at the marriage ceremony, or even to wear one to show off your status, but most brides joyfully go along with the tide of tradition, not looking so much for a fashion item but for a symbol of lasting appeal and attraction that they will wear to the end of their days. So it is important to take time choosing, not to leave a decision to the last moment. What do you need to think about?

What style do you want – how original and how intricate? Is it to be a plain gold band, or twists, chains, interlocking segments, a garland of orange blossoms? You will need to consider design in relation to durability and to the carat of the metal – and, of course, to cost.

Is your ring going to be ready made or specially designed?

Is it to be new, old or antique? If it is antique, VAT is not levied.

Do you want gold or platinum? If you choose gold, which alloy will you specify, since this gives very different colours to the finished product?

How wide do you want the band?

What size do you need? You can find out by using a ring gauge, but you do need to be realistic and bear in mind that your joints may swell when you get older.

What sort of finish do you want – molten, satin or burnished?

Do you intend to wear it with your engagement ring? Two different metals look odd together, and interact if one is harder than the other, as indeed do two rings of different carat. Does the stone of your engagement ring 'sit' comfortably on your wedding ring?

Are you both going to wear wedding rings, a matching pair?

Do you want engraving inside your rings, initials maybe, or a simple message? Check whether there is an extra charge for this – as well as for any alterations you may need.

Does it make you happy to receive your ring in an elaborate 'free' presentation case? If this pleases you, fine, but do not be taken in by anything labelled 'free'. What will you do with the case – you will not be using it to keep your ring in? Is a simple white pouch enough?

Consider the question of insurance, again sometimes offered 'free'. You may as well take it, but when the renewal comes up, transfer any jewelry to your house contents policy, on which you may have to specify items over a certain value. It is cheaper that way.

The wedding ring plays a central part in the wedding ceremony. Yet when choosing even this traditional and symbolic item, you will find that there are many alternative styles to choose from.

COACH, CARRIAGE, WHEELBARROW, MUDCART

'Get me to the church on time' – how you do it is your own affair, whether you choose boat, bus or butcher's bike, milk-float or school minibus, stage coach or carriage and pair, vintage Rolls or sleek black limousine, dustcart or donkey. The more spectacular your transport, the more likely you are to get your picture in the papers. But there is always a niggling doubt: the only certain way of being in complete control over your arrival at the ceremony is on your own two feet. And even then . . . Lynn had lived in the village all her life and she intended to have a mediaeval marriage procession from home to church, and on to the Women's Institute for her reception. But just as she was putting the finishing touches to her veil, down came the rain. Undeterred by the downpour, Lynn went off to her wedding in white wellington boots, and swathed in an outsize plastic bag. She had lovely laughing photographs to cherish, and memories of a myriad of multi-coloured umbrellas bobbing along the muddy lane behind her.

The criteria for choosing your transport fall into two groups: the purely practical, and the very personal. Practically, it is the means of moving people round from place to place, it is convenient, it saves time – barring breakdowns and bolting horses – it provides protection from blustery winds and drenching rain, and it offers you a few brief moments of peace and privacy. Personally, it gives you the chance to indulge yourself, to ride for the first time in a Silver Cloud, to feel like a princess waving elegantly to the neighbours as you pass on and out of their lives; or to counterbalance the seriousness of the ceremony with the fun and frivolity of Dad trundling you along in a traditional wooden, well-scrubbed wheelbarrow; or to demonstrate publicly the sharing of your husband's life, by leaving the reception in the furniture van which is his livelihood.

It is your choice entirely, although, like any other service, transport is subject to availability, and your stage-coach and liveried horsemen may have to be booked as much as a year in advance.

FROM FANTASY TO PRACTICALITY

Substantial numbers of people are going to be on the move, and they will not be joining you in flights of fancy. You need to work out your commitments for transport to the church or register office for yourself and your father, your mother and the bridesmaids – with a surreptitious check on how the best man proposes to get your bridegroom to the ceremony on time. Afterwards, you will both require a 'conveyance' to get you to the reception, with cars for the best man and bridesmaids and for the parents. So, very basic needs seem to be two to three cars for the bridal party, with additions for older or handicapped people. These cars do not have to be hired; if you are on a strict budget you can probably find friends and relatives willing to take over, if you are prepared to descend from the Daimler league; and you will certainly find many car owners who are quite happy to take those who do not drive from ceremony to reception. On the other hand, you may wish to discourage driving altogether so that there are no problems over drink: you can hire a minibus – or even a red London bus to transport everyone to the reception.

PITFALLS AND PROBLEMS

You may sometimes take a taxi, but there are not many occasions when you need a chauffeur-driven car. So how do you find a firm you can rely on? Although you can use the *Yellow Pages*, small ads, or a hotel's all-in package deal, it is a personal recommendation that really counts. Only someone who has used a service can honestly appraise it, and comment on the standard of driving: whether it was a sickening stop, start, shooting-through-the-red-lights experience.

You would not want to use Fred's firm, for example. Fred crawled out rather huffily from under the car he was servicing, gave his hands a quick wipe on an oily rag and stripped off his overalls. He was late for that wedding already. The traffic turned out to be worse than usual and Diana was dithering about on the doorstep when, in a gleaming black Daimler Majestic Major, he arrived wearing – a brilliant Fairisle sweater. And there he remained in his driver's seat with his black-rimmed finger-nails, gripping the wheel; he had no intention whatsoever of opening the car door for the bride. 'I'm a mechanic,' he muttered, 'not a bloody chauffeur.' Diana, undaunted, reminded herself that some brides actually paid deliberately dirty chimney sweeps to bring them luck, and here she was with a – albeit uncooperative – Fred free with her package.

Though there are many highly reputable companies that give you real red carpet treatment, you do have to be on the alert when you are choosing. Chauffeur-driven cars are owned either by private individuals, or by firms that are not licensed like taxis and therefore cannot ply for hire in the streets or use public taxi ranks. As all their journeys are fixed bookings, you will have to make your arrangements through an office, which may be attached to a garage. Whereas taxi drivers have to pass strict tests set by their local authority, have their vehicles vetted and their fare rates fixed, there are far fewer official controls for chauffeur-driven cars. Apart from legally complying with MOT roadworthiness and licensing arrangements, the standards they set are in most cases their own. These can be very high, but they can also slip. Moreover, there is always the risk of a small firm going out of business between your booking and being married – perhaps even disappearing with your deposit.

LOOKING AND CHECKING

You will need to get several estimates before you come to a final decision, and these are the kinds of questions you might want to ask:

What types, styles and colours of cars do they have for hire? Do any of these appeal to you?

Can you see them? How spacious are they, particularly important if you have a long train or hooped gown? How clean are they, especially their upholstery?

Can you make a booking for the day and time and for the number of people you need to transport? How many cars does this involve?

How much will it cost? How do they work it out: on a mileage or time basis, or on a combination of the two? Is VAT included?

What is the system for deposit, cancellation and final payment? How can possibly embarrassing situations involving money on the wedding day be avoided?

What sort of decorations will the cars have? Will the bridal car have flowers, ribbons, nylon net?

What does the chauffeur wear – chauffeur's uniform, peaked cap, suit, or Fairisle sweater?

Is the car you will use wired for music? How good is the sound reproduction? What is the repertoire? Can you choose not to have music without hurting anyone's feelings?

Have all the drivers got clean licences? Are they first and foremost chauffeurs, or are they doing double duty as mechanics?

There are moments when even a white Rolls Royce has to take second place.

'*The chance of a lifetime.*' *A deliberately-contrived pose may seem over the top, but your wedding day is a once-in-a-lifetime chance to have some unusual and stunning photographs taken of yourself.*

FOR THE RECORD –
PHOTOS, PICTURES AND PORTRAITS

Wendy and Walter went on waiting, looking in vain on the doormat each morning for the delivery of their wedding snaps. One of their friends who rather fancied himself as a David Bailey with his Olympus OM 1 had taken lots of informal shots of their wedding, seventy-two more pictures for them to treasure, they thought. Arthur had sent off his two rolls for processing the day after the wedding, but they were never seen again. No record of Wendy stepping into her dress, putting the finishing touches to her veil, laughing at the family cat curled up asleep on her train, giving her bouquet to her great-grandmother with a loving kiss . . . Nothing. Nothing but some financial compensation – much more in fact than the original cost of the films and their postage – because their friend, Arthur, had done three important things:

He had kept details about the films he had sent away, their type, number of exposures, the content of each one, the date of posting and the name and address of the firm;

He had remembered to include Wendy's and Walter's correct name and address in clear writing;

He had written a covering letter, keeping a carbon copy, pointing out the unique, irreplaceable content of the two rolls of film.

Wendy and Walter would also have got compensation if their prints, transparencies or negatives had been damaged, or if Wendy's mother had appeared with a large black spot on her nose: any service you use must be carried out in 'a proper and workmanlike manner', taking reasonable care and using suitable materials. So there is no reason, whatever sort of record you choose, whether prints, portraits, slides, 8mm colour film or video cassette, for you to accept second-rate service from any professional: Lorna went in for a video recording, for which she had agreed to pay £150 for coverage of her ceremony and reception, but the technician had not come to terms with his equipment and managed somehow to wipe out all the churchyard scenes. 'We could never, never put this right', Lorna wept – and deducted £75 from her final bill. She was quite within her legal rights to make a deduction for loss of services and a much valued product, and to atone for her acute disappointment – though the actual amount might be a subject for dispute. In her case it was not.

But if Arthur, who had no commercial contract with Wendy and Walter, had gone round taking photos that chopped off heads, enlarged feet and got faces out of focus, that would have been a different matter. It is one of the greatest risks you take with D-I-Y photography: it is fine as a supplement, particularly as the means of achieving informal and even intimate pictures, and it is certainly a way of saving money if you are hard up. But in the first instance it is best to rely on a real professional who is more likely than any amateur to be able to cope with swift changes of film at crucial moments, failure of equipment, bad weather and tricky lighting conditions. Most brides do in fact choose a professional, even if it is only for a basic order, as a greater guarantee of security.

FIRST THOUGHTS ON PHOTOGRAPHS

How do you want to preserve your wedding for posterity, and for your own delight?

Do you want black and white prints, which are suitable for passing on to newspapers and house magazines, as well as colour prints? Do you want a matt or glossy finish?

Do you want these professionally presented in an album or as separate items for you to arrange yourself, as mounted prints, as enlargements, and your special favourite as a canvas-bonded portrait?

Do you want your proofs developed quickly and passed round during the reception, running the risk of making your guests feel pressurized into purchase?

Do you want a studio portrait which can be taken before the wedding?

Do you want an 8mm colour film, video cassette or even tape recording, perhaps using your own suggestions for titles to provide the structure you would like?

And how do all your 'wants' fit in with the money you have set aside for record-keeping?

It is also important at this early stage to give your mind to the mixture of formality and informality that you would like, in order to build up a step-by-step account of your wedding as it really was. If you do not want pictures of a large number of guests posing, leave them off the list of priorities you give to your photographer. Consider putting a limit, too, on the number of shots of speechmakers in action, particularly as bulbs flashing in faces are unnerving.

Where do you want your pictures taken? You will have to be quite clear as to whether you want your photographer at your home, the reception, ceremony and final departure. The choice is yours, depending on what you want to spend, with one exception: the ceremony. It is the clergyman who has the final say about allowing photographs and video recordings in his church. It may be that he objects only to flash and floodlights, or it may be a matter of irrevocable personal principle. This is a subject to raise at an early stage, and you must accept his decision without question.

Do check that you finally get from your professional everything you have agreed on. If you are told – or better still, have it clearly set down in writing – that there will be 'complete coverage of your wedding at church and reception', and the photographer slips away as soon as all the guests have been received, this constitutes breach of contract. In addition the Trade Descriptions . . . might have been broken, if the photographer or his firm makes this sort of statement in advertisements and brochures.

Do you have any special requirements? You are likely to want a sequence of pictures that tell a story, but you might also want to consider a series of special effects (do these cost extra?), where you need to understand what is available: you can have, for example, superimposed photographs, perhaps a picture of the bridal couple inset into an interior shot of the church; or you can have 'misties', that is, photographs taken with a soft lens to give a dreamy, romantic feeling – notice how often this technique is used in television and magazine advertisements for cosmetics, perfumes, and indeed any product where the appeal is emotional; you can have close-ups not just of loving looks and lights in your eyes but pictures of two hands, fingers entwined, showing off two shining gold wedding rings resting on a crimson velvet or white satin cushion. Definitely not for those who gnaw their nails. Or you can have your close-ups outlined in hearts, horseshoes and wishbones, be-ribboned with love knots, or with their definition fading out gently into a soft mingling of pastel shades. You can be as fantastic as you like, but take a look first at existing examples of the art of wedding photography to see what attracts you most. Finally, face up to the fact that there may be difficult situations within your family that you do not want to feature or perpetuate in your photographs. Are there any particular factions or known 'separatist movements' – which you will also have to watch over if you are drawing up seating plans for your reception? Apart from problems of divorce or separation, where differences can often be submerged or subdued just for your own special day, every family and its mixed bag of friends and relations will have its list of acknowledged incompatibilities and conflicting interests. All these will have to be tactfully admitted and accepted in your instructions to your photographer.

CHOOSING A PHOTOGRAPHER

You can consult friends who have recently got married and whose judgment you trust, and you can look at the evidence of their albums; or you can look at the *Yellow Pages* and your local papers, scanning the advertisements for photographers who specialize in weddings. You may find that, as soon as news of your engagement gets round through official announcements, you are bombarded by brochures and confronted by door-to-door salesmen; you can be particularly vulnerable within the greater intimacy of your own home, especially when a visit comes as a complete surprise. Take care not to commit yourself, and never sign anything on the spur of the moment. Have a good look at what else is on offer. You will certainly want more than one quotation, but you may find that it is extremely difficult to compare like with like since services vary: you may, for example, find a firm offering a day rate at a fixed price with a set number of pictures – perhaps sixty – out of which you choose twenty for an album; and you may find another, which offers a price for each finished photograph but with no daily booking charge. Make sure you know exactly what is included in the deal – whether you can keep the proofs, whether they are overstamped so that they are worthless to you, who actually owns the copyright and the negatives – how long they are kept on file, and what sort of time limit there is before the price goes up. Only by looking around at your leisure will you get the feel of the market and an idea of what constitutes value for money. Certainly give special consideration to a local photographer since he – or she – will not need to charge you for travelling time, and he will know the locality and how to avoid going off to the wrong church or wrong reception in cases where names are similar. He will be familiar with lighting conditions, and with the artistic possibilities of churchyards, grounds and gardens; he will know the policy of ministers with regard to photographs; he will have established contacts with the local press, and can in fact be a mine of information about all sorts of adjacent aspects of weddings.

MAKING YOUR BOOKING

You may turn out to be the one who is rejected, because the first favourite on your list of photographers is already booked up. But if you do have a choice, before finally committing yourself and your deposit to anyone, make sure you meet the person who will actually carry out the job at your wedding, not just the manager. It matters very much whether you like him as a person, whether you feel natural in his presence, whether he brings out the sparkle and not the sulks, whether he understands and appreciates your requirements, which will be emotional as well as rational. He is going to be your stage manager for the record, gently but firmly organizing large numbers of people, manoeuvring and manipulating them so that they appear at their best. Many bridegrooms spoil pictures for posterity by standing sloppily, and droopily displaying to disadvantage the clothes they have chosen so carefully for the occasion! Find out too if your photographer is a full-time professional, what qualifications he has, whether his work has ever been selected for a nationwide exhibition – and look at examples to see if you like his style. Ask who processes his films and prints his photographs, as many 'professionals' contract out their processing nowadays. And discuss emergency arrangements with him: what happens in high winds and heavy rains? What if his flash unit fails? And what if he falls ill on the day?

Only now are you in a position to make your final decision, getting written confirmation in due course about the times and places you have stipulated, with clear addresses for home, ceremony and reception, and details of the basic fee, price of prints, consequent extras and enlargements. You should be clear about the terms of your deposit if you have to cancel, and about arrangements for viewing proofs and paying the final bill. It is a good idea to get your own order in early – often at a lower price – before you pass proofs round to your relatives, as it can take ages to get their order together. And do be tactful and clear about who pays!

HISTORY AS IT HAPPENS

A couple of days before your wedding check that everything is in order, just in case you have to make a last-minute substitution. Provide a final written timetable of events, not only for your photographer, but also for a close friend who can be briefed as liaison 'man' to help round up and group any necessary friends and members of the family. Among your 'top ten' pictures you will certainly want to consider including:

The groom and best man when they arrive;

The bridesmaids and bride's mother;

The bride and her father;

The bridal couple signing the register;

The couple coming out of church;

The couple getting into their car;

Receiving guests at the reception;

Cutting the cake;

Proposing the toast;

Leaving for the honeymoon.

Allow plenty of time in your plans for photographs, perhaps about five minutes when you arrive at the church for quick, informal, windswept shots, but longer for arrangement of veils and trains and catching little bridesmaids who play hide and seek behind gravestones; about twenty minutes after the ceremony, and just as long as it takes at the reception. Some photographers want to be up and off once the reception is under way, and even rig the cake cutting ceremony to speed their departure. Make sure in advance that this is acceptable and that any curtailment of service is considered in the price you pay. And if the photographer does stay until your departure, do feed him.

LETTING PEOPLE KNOW: ANNOUNCEMENTS AND INVITATIONS

Paula heard the paper-boy, whistling out of tune as usual, long before she saw him. She rushed out to the front gate and almost snatched the *Wentworth Gazette* from him. Here at last in black and white she would see their names publicly linked together, she would really be convinced that tomorrow she would be married to Peter. She spread out the pages on the kitchen table careless of the breakfast crumbs. Here it was: Births, Marriages and Deaths. Fingers trembling, eyes hard to focus at first. Where was it – that announcement she had so carefully worded with Peter? She knew it by heart.

> 'The marriage will take place' – were they tempting Providence, they had wondered – 'between Peter, only son of Mr and Mrs L. H. Faithful of 12 The Pathway, Wentforth, and Paula, younger daughter of Mr and Mrs B. Doughty of 41 Beaumont Avenue, Wentworth, at St Stephen's Church at 11.30 a.m. on April 7th.'

But it just was not there. There was no mistake – other brides were getting married on Saturday; their news was there for all to see. But not hers. She was about to stump off angrily to the telephone to tell the editor of the *Wentworth Gazette* exactly what she thought of his paper when her eye fell on the small print:

> 'Family notices: announcements within these columns cannot be accepted without the signature and address of the author as a guarantee of authenticity. Notices must arrive by second post Tuesday for the Friday issue.'

Certainly both she and Peter had signed their announcement to prove that it was genuine, but when had they actually posted it off? There had been so much to do and she could not think very clearly. It had been the day she collected the cake, and that was Tuesday. Too late, she realized now. But she would be in good time for their next communication. Out came her pen. Marriages section this time, actual and not just forthcoming, she thought – tempting Providence again, writing defiantly:

> 'Faithful: Doughty – on April 7th at St Stephen's Church, Peter David Faithful to Paula Jane Doughty, daughter of Mr and Mrs Brian Doughty of Wentworth.'

When the boy delivered the following week's paper, Paula was no longer at home. Providence had not been tempted.

IN THE NEWS

You may be like Paula and Peter and prefer a 'forthcoming marriage' announcement – being very wary about timing – to one proclaiming your engagement. And, like them, you may, if you have both lived and even worked in the same town for a long time, choose to concentrate on your local press rather than going to the much greater expense of advertising in *The Times* or *Telegraph*. It all depends on the nature of your family and your circle of friends. And you may wish to consider the *Gazettes* and *Gleaners* of other countries if your connections lie there. But what else do you want besides a straight announcement? You may be shy, shun publicity, and want to keep everything very private. Nevertheless, a wedding is historically a public affair with the calling of banns, and even declarations in the market-place in days gone by. Nowadays a wedding in a register office still has to be 'with open doors', which means that technically the whole population has the right to try to cram itself in; moreover, the Superintendent Registrar's book of forthcoming marriages is there for people to look at and a notice is displayed on his board. But unless you are a pop star or sports personality, nobody is going to take much interest. However, if you want a little publicity, there are certain things you can do:

Make sure that a suitable – preferably black and white – photograph reaches your newspapers, not forgetting the free press. There will be no charge for this as you will be 'news'. Photographers often have direct contacts with the local papers, and your photographer will be able to send in your picture if you complete a special form. You can also alert the press yourself so that they have the chance to send along a photographer of their own;

Tell your local papers about your wedding so that they can send a reporter to interview you; or you can write up your own version, remembering that all essentials must be contained in a few lively sentences;

Send an account to your house journal or magazine at work, to the newsletter of a society, organization or old school association that you belong to – editors of these will be just as glad to have copy as those of glossy society magazines;

Do something unusual at your wedding, but do not let sensationalism get out of character: fulfil a wish, exploit a fantasy – arrive in your great-uncle's bull-nosed Morris, in a sleigh with jingling bells, even on roller-skates, depart in a helicopter, hovercraft or haywain. Involve other people – like the couple who went to camp on honeymoon with the local cub pack;

Check with the minister of your church that news of your marriage will duly appear in the parish magazine.

This wedding reception was held in beautiful surroundings, and the photographer took full advantage of them when photographing the bride and groom.

INVITING PEOPLE

You may want the world at large to know your news and to share your joy, and you will certainly want your family and friends to participate in the ceremony and celebration. You want them to be with you, close to you, supporting you on this most meaningful of days. So, a good six weeks before your wedding, out go your invitations – you can use second class post – normally sent in your parent's name. Paula and Peter worked on the wording:

Mr and Mrs Brian Doughty
request the pleasure of the company of
. . . .
at the marriage of their daughter
Paula Jane
to
Mr Peter David Faithful
at St Stephen's Church, Wentworth
on Saturday, April 7th 1984
at 11.30 a.m.
and at a reception afterwards at
the Montrose Hotel

41 Beaumont Avenue,
Wentworth
R.S.V.P.

They argued a bit about leaving a space for the names of the guests: Peter thought they could just say 'the pleasure of your company' to everyone, whereas Paula maintained that people's names would have to appear somewhere and that her clear italic script would look better in a special space rather than randomly written at the top. They looked at several samples of invitations and finally settled for silver cursive lettering on thick white card with crinkly edges, decorated with a border of tiny wedding bells. She and Peter had also considered gold print, black print, even navy blue print, on a variety of different coloured cards, some of them single, some folded, some shiny, some matt, in many different styles and print sizes and with many different motifs and decorations. A bewildering array, but as the local stationer told her, 'We have all this large number of designs, and yet it's funny how couples all seem to go for the same two or three in the end.'

They put in their order about three months before their wedding even though the manager assured Paula that everything was always ready within two to three weeks. She made certain, too, that her own 'penalty clause' was added: 'This order is needed by January 31st 1984 at the latest'. 'Time is of the essence', she muttered to herself, 'but I'd better say it more simply to make sure they get the message.' She had also taken the precaution of typing out the wording, checking the fine detail of names, addresses and times down to St Stephen's apostrophe and full stops beside R.S.V.P. She thought it was rather strange to go on using this archaic French abbreviation for 'Répondez s'il vous plaît': why couldn't they say 'Please reply'? But there it was; she was being very traditional and she did want people to reply quickly so that she could send invitations to those on the reserve list when refusals came in. She reckoned on a 10 per cent 'failure' rate, and that for the 100 guests they intended to invite, they would need 75 invitations in the first place since many of them were couples. So a print run of 100 should leave her with plenty to spare; after all, the laying out and setting up constitutes the main cost, not the printing of a few extra copies.

What alternatives are there to ordering from a stationer, as Paula and Peter did, choosing from a large selection displayed in a demonstration album? Your choice depends on your attitudes to individuality, originality and tradition, possibly on your own artistic ability, and certainly on your budget. You could consider:

Using thick white blank cards and matching envelopes from a general office stationers, writing your own wording in black ink using a real pen, decorated according to your interest and ability – perhaps with dried pressed flowers, or manipulating motifs and interlinking letraset initials. You can even make a monogram on the back flap of the envelope;

Buying packets of mass-produced cards for you to fill in yourself, in silver or in colour from specialist card shops and stationers. These are also useful as spares if you miscalculate the quantity for a printed order;

Employing a local printer: for most people this is the only time in their lives when they actually contemplate coping with a printer – and become aware of the possibilities of new technology. Off-set litho can be used to produce, at speed, traditional invitations complete with hearts, horseshoes and wedding bells, or unusual effects such as a mediaeval parchment scroll which you can tie up with ribbon and a red seal;

Consulting a specialist artist and engraver who will produce original designs and drawings to make your invitations not only very personal but also real works of art.

CAKE AND COMPLIMENTS

Though it will be your mother who cuts up your cake into chunks to send away in little boxes to people who were not able to be present at your wedding, it will be your responsibility to prepare your compliments cards – which do double duty as change-of-address cards. You can have supplies of these printed in silver with your maiden name in the top lefthand corner crossed through with an arrow, or you can buy small, blank visiting cards and envelopes which you fill in for yourself.

Once more Paula took up her pen, with a fine italic nib:

Mr and Mrs Peter D. Faithful,
The Haven,
5 Paradise Way,
Wentworth
With compliments on the occasion of their wedding
April 7th 1984

This is the first time I am writing 'Mr and Mrs Faithful', she thought, dreaming of the days that were to come. Then she went to buy grease-proof paper to cut into little squares to protect her cards from the cake.

CONCLUSION

Paula, with her cake, compliments cards and packets of grease-proof paper, combines in her attitudes and actions the romance and realism, the poetry and practicality which are the twin themes at the heart of this book. Neither is complete without the other in that vast, complex and unfamiliar experience of arranging and organizing a wedding. The one balances the other – but it is a balance which cannot be achieved without effort, information and awareness, and indeed self-knowledge. It is easy for any bride to wallow in emotion, conditioned by circumstance, by 'what the songs sing about, poets write about and advertisements tell you about'. However, it is hard to apportion the amount of emotional luxury you are going to allow yourself; hard to collect and classify, sift and screen all the information needed for effective organization – based in the last resort on your own taste and values.

Choosing is never without its problems: sometimes you find yourself in a situation where you have no choice, constrained perhaps by laws, regulations and requirements – even by time itself; or the choice may not be yours to make, as in the case of Susan who could not get married in the church about which she had always dreamed. More often, choice turns out to be a compromise born of conflict and co-operation within the family framework, or a practical solution to a problem – often financial – as to how you match up what you want with what you have got. Often, when real choice exists, the possibilities are endless, which means that you have to gather in a very large amount of information, made more difficult because frequently the facts are shrouded in unfamiliar and specialist language. You have to assess what is right for you: which menu, which music, which photographer, which florist ... where to go on honeymoon, where indeed to live happily ever after.

To help you, this book includes background material based on real-life stories, and lots of check-lists to start you thinking about the things that matter most to you and the questions you could be considering. It will also remind you of all that needs to be done, often in a short space of time; and it suggests techniques, such as pairing and rating, to help you through bewildering complex choices. In addition, it should inspire you to add your own ideas to the creation of your unique event.

Choice also involves challenge: if you cannot do or have one thing, what else is possible? This book – about real brides and real weddings – features many misfortunes and mishaps, problems and pitfalls, with not a single occasion irretrievably spoiled. For, though it gives glimpses of fears and frustrations, tears and even anger, it also shows examples of opportunities seized: for the creative conversion of calamities; for ingenuity and imagination, originality and enterprise, resourcefulness and self-reliance; for co-operation and community involvement.

Above all, it shows how to look back with laughter and with love.

There is no knowing what your friends may spring on you at your wedding. This unusual guard of honour from the bride and groom's music-hall group took them completely by surprise as they came out of the church.

'It's a new beginning, a chance to start again, but this time it's sharing.'

INDEX